Y0-CLH-831

Papal Paganism

By J. A. PHILLIPS

Author of "Roman Catholicism Analyzed," "Catholic
Intolerance," and "The Romish Position
on Marriage"

DISCARD

COKESBURY PRESS

NASHVILLE, TENN

1924

COPYRIGHT, 1924
BY
LAMAR & BARTON

PREFATORY NOTE

SURROUNDED as we are with the forms of Christianity, and feeling that the claims of Jesus Christ are to a considerable degree recognized by the most of our fellow-citizens, we of the United States—and of Europe as well—may easily forget that at least two-thirds of the human race are as fully under the sway of idolatry, superstition, priestcraft, and their attendant evils as they were at the beginning of the Christian era.

If Christianity, after nineteen centuries, has been able to give a measure of freedom and joy to only 500,000,000 people, we have cause for heart searchings. Have we nothing to do with the more than a billion souls who know nothing of our Christ? World Courts, Hague Tribunals, Leagues of Nations, Peace Plans, etc., are only symptoms of a desire for world peace. None of these things can do much; the implanting of a deep desire to practice voluntarily the principles of justice, kindness, and the love of God is paramount.

During the first four centuries after Christ there were aspirations for the evangelization of the world. At the beginning of the nineteenth century, this vision burst again on the view of Christendom. Why should the world be deprived of the Sun of Righteousness for eleven hundred years? Christianity barely lived in Europe; that continent was only in a measure preserved. Asia, Africa, and Australia were practically untouched.

Now that science, wealth, philosophy, liberty, and power are largely concentrated in the hands of the nominally Christian nations, we face the most tremendous responsibility of all the ages. How shall we meet it? In our efforts to understand world problems shall we ignore Romanism?

The Roman Catholic religion deserves the same careful examination which any other system of thought and conduct deserves. Three lines of investigation are indispensable if we would comprehend its real nature: (1) Its present-day practices and purposes; (2) its history and the fruits of its history; (3) its authoritative doctrines.

To ignore Rome's unquenchable thirst for world power and her utter intolerance of the rights of all other religions is sheer folly.

We may reasonably expect Romanism to be on its good behavior in the United States; therefore, the indelible marks of that system which are found in this country are infallible indexes to her world program and indicate the mere beginnings and mildest forms of her doctrines and propaganda.

Strenuous, well-organized efforts are being made to make America Catholic. By missions to non-Catholics, immigration of Romanists, parochial schools, books and papers, hospital service, and pretensions to Americanism, the hierarchies of Italy and the United States have been, for more than a half-century, endeavoring to swing religion, politics, and morality to the Vatican. That their scheme is partially successful is evident. The simple fact that more than half of our Protestants are averse to the study of Romanism shows the drift. Ignorance of

Catholicism is regarded by many almost as if it were a passport into *élite* society.

A bill was introduced into our Congress and Senate in December, 1923, making it unlawful for any organization to have legal recognition which "shall attempt to bring into disrepute, infringe, embarrass, hamper, or interfere with any religion or religious belief, or the practice thereof . . . or shall publish, or cause to be published in a newspaper or magazine devoted exclusively to that purpose, any threatening, harmful, insidious, or inciting statements of a comprehensive and general nature, against any religion, or the profession and practice thereof." The very fact that such a Roman Catholic law could even be proposed to the great lawmaking body of our democratic government is in itself enough to cause alarm.

The Catholic press is bolder, more anti-American, unscrupulous, defiant, and influential now than it has ever been in our history. A prominent Catholic paper (issue of November 25, 1923) makes this statement: "Eliminate the 5,000,000 negroes who are listed as Protestants, and the total Protestant affiliation will not be greater than the total Catholic membership." H. K. Carroll, the Church statistician, gives Rome 15,500,000. The above-mentioned paper would make it more than 40,000,000. While such exaggerated statements are ridiculous to those who know, they are yet calculated to inflame several millions of Catholics with the idea that America is soon to be Catholic. A certain weekly paper, whose Catholic proclivities are kept under cover, regales the public continually with a recital of the dissensions and weakness of Protestant Churches, with never a hint or a word as to the intrinsic evils of Romanism.

In 1858 the society of the Paulist Fathers was organized in this country for the purpose of adapting Romanism to America. In the course of time a book, "Question Box Answers," was put out by them with the intent to deceive the American people concerning real Romanism. The 1921 edition indicates that 2,000,000 copies have been issued. "The Faith of Our Fathers," by Cardinal Gibbons, uses the same tactics and has reached perhaps even a larger circulation. On account of these and similar efforts Rome claims to have made many thousands of converts.

The stubborn fact that Rome has not changed and cannot change is clearly stated by Pope Leo XIII. in an encyclical addressed to Cardinal Gibbons under date of January 22, 1899. He there refers to the effort to Americanize Romanism and says: "It requires, certainly, no long discussion, beloved son, to show that this whole scheme is wrong." The periodical effort to bring about union between Anglicanism and the Papacy, and especially its uniform failure, only emphasizes what every student of Romanism knows. The methods of the hierarchy in dealing with Austria, Spain, Hungary, Bolivia, Peru, Ecuador, the Philippines, Southern Ireland, and Italy, during the closing years of the nineteenth and the beginning of the twentieth century, prove that the medieval dogma of papal supremacy over civil government, with all the degradation which that entails, has not abated in the least.

The estimate Lord Macaulay gave of Romanism is still true. He says:

> It is impossible to deny that the polity of the Church of Rome is the very masterpiece of human wisdom. In truth nothing but such a polity could, against such assaults, have borne up such doctrines. The experience of twelve hundred eventful years, the ingenuity and patient care of forty generations of statesmen, have improved that polity to such perfection that, among the contrivances which have been devised for deceiving and oppressing mankind, it occupies the highest place.[1]

Has the pope ceased at any time to curse and misrepresent the work of Bible societies, the Y. M. C. A., the activities of Protestants in the city of Rome, State education, liberty of worship, private interpretation of Scripture, civil marriage, or government of, for, and by the people?

The fact that Romanism has always stood for all the vital things in paganism is so striking that a careful study of its origin is now imperative. In tracing that religion back to Italy several centuries before Christ, we shall be able to get a consistent philosophy of it. Certain it is that we have not been able successfully to meet the contentions of the hierarchy on any other hypothesis. For some strange reason or reasons our theologians have usually overlooked the ingrained heathenism of the papacy inherited from old pagan Rome and which is essential to her very life.

As soon as we meet the Roman question in the

---

[1]Essay on Von Ranke.

heroic spirit of Jesus Christ we shall be ready to give
to the world the gospel; until then we shall continue
to spend much time haggling and continue to get
only a little way toward the establishment of God's
kingdom among men.   J. A. PHILLIPS.

PHŒNIX, ARIZ., April 1, 1924.

CONTENTS

INTRODUCTION

THE innocent Protestant who picks up this little book will probably ask such questions as the following: Is not this an attack on sincere Catholics? Is it right to unsettle the faith of good people? Would it not be better to spend our time in building up rather than tearing down; in preaching the gospel instead of fighting Romanism? Should we oppose an institution that has done so much good in the United States and in the world? If the Catholic Church is doing some good, ought we not to let it alone and bid it Godspeed? Ought we to slander people who are doing the best they can? Is not the Catholic religion worth something in controlling the ignorant? Is there not some good in Romanism? Does not the Catholic Church accept the fundamentals—as, *e. g.*, the Bible, the deity of Christ, the trinity, the work of the Holy Spirit, etc.? Has not the Catholic the same right to defend his religion that Protestants have to defend theirs? Ought we not to try to coöperate with all good Catholics instead of fighting them? Do Catholic priests attack Protestantism? Can one who has never been a Catholic understand Catholicism? How can we criticize a religion which builds hospitals, parochial schools, orphan homes, homes for the aged, and furnishes sisters of charity for the relief of suffering? Do all Catholics accept the infamous doctrines taught by their theologians?

I answer:

This is not an attack on Catholics, but a careful study of Catholicism. Protestants have studied Mormonism, Mohammedanism, Buddhism, Confucianism, etc. How does it happen that we are to be forbidden to study Romanism? Who told us we should not or must not? Is not that a new application of Rome's attack on liberty of worship, of conscience, of thought, of the press? And who is making such a plea for the Romish right of secrecy? Is it not Romanized Protestants?

Although one may be personally a conscientious Catholic, he is yet in some measure responsible for the doctrines and policy of his religion; if those are wrong, it is not his faith in God that is to be unsettled, but his blind confidence in his Church. If an unsuspecting Protestant thinks for a moment that his "good Catholic neighbor" would not harm him, let him put that "good Catholic neighbor" to the test in a community which is controlled by Romish influence.

To one of the Old Testament worthies (Jer. i. 10) it was given to "root out, and to pull down, and to destroy, and to throw down, to build, and to plant." Jesus said that he came not to bring peace on the earth, but a sword. The Apostle Paul disturbed the faith of hundreds of sincere people; indeed his own faith had to be demolished before he could forsake his bloody creed. The same apostle taught us to "abhor that which is evil." Europe has advanced because of her conflicts; Asia has remained stagnant for lack of them. Besides, the least effort to give Scripture truth to Catholics is always interfered with

by meddlesome priests. This forces us to set forth the unscriptural character of Romanism. If the gospel is preached, sin must be rebuked. Why should a Christian exempt Romanism, for instance, in his fight on gambling, or the liquor traffic, or cheating, or anti-patriotic schemes? Since the Roman Catholic Church is definitely committed to gambling, the liquor traffic, cheating, and union of Church and State (as will be proven later), it would be foolish for us to attack those sins and refuse to show that a so-called religion with twenty thousand priests in this country is giving to them all virtually its solid support.

Has the Catholic Church done good in this country and in all the world? Has the good she has done outweighed the evil? Suppose a goodly majority of every country were Catholic; would it be good for the rest of the world? How does it happen that Romanism seems to be good in Protestant countries while it is an unmitigated evil in Catholic countries? Can we bid any system Godspeed whose ultimate aim is to destroy the liberty of those who place the New Testament, privately interpreted, above such claims as the pope makes and above such a history as Rome has made in illustration of those claims? Many gamblers and saloon men have done good, many of them have tender hearts, many of them relieve suffering; shall we therefore not oppose the liquor traffic and gambling? There are many good Mohammedans and Buddhists; shall we therefore not study the character of those cults?

Do we slander a man because we try to cure him

of hookworm and endeavor to remove the cause of its transmission to those who do not have it?

The Catholic Church does control the ignorant by keeping them in ignorance or by deceiving them as to the fundamentals of their own religion. But the same force that controls them—that is, the hierarchy —also incites them to riot and murder.

Is there not some good in Romanism? Yes; just as there is some good in other pagan cults or even in atheism. For instance, atheists hold that we should guard our health by work, sleep, and good food.

The teaching body of the Catholic Church cannot teach the fundamentals. Their Bible is more than neutralized by being placed on a level with tradition and by vicious translations and explanatory notes. The Catholic Jesus is responsible for all the wickedness which is taught *authoritatively* and for all the diabolical *commands* given forth by his vicar while acting as pope. Therefore he is not the Christ of Christianity. The Catholic Holy Spirit is supposed to be poured on the faithful by means of the magical power of confirmation—an utterly false assumption. And, since the clergy teach with *full* authority, their holy spirit is a most unholy spirit. The Catholic trinity is made up of a wicked father, a Jesus who authorizes the sins and crimes taught by the priests, and an unholy spirit who permits the Holy Bible to be kept away from the people.

All Catholics have a right to defend their religion. But that is not what they are contending for; their thesis is that no human being has any right to throw any light on the ungodly essentials of Romanism. The right for which Romanists contend is the right to prevent Protestants and liberals from showing the untenableness of Romanism.

To coöperate with a good Catholic in religious matters is impossible. To coöperate with a good man who is in the Catholic Church, but who hates the basic principles of Romanism, is a very practical thing and is often done.

That Catholic priests attack Protestantism most viciously is demonstrated wherever they can debauch their members. It is set forth also in their literature.

A non-Catholic can understand Romanism as well as a physician can understand the smallpox without having it.

Do the sisters who care for the sick, the orphans, and the aged in Catholic institutions submit to the demands of the priests, the pope, and the theologians? If so, it is their duty to make propaganda superior to good deeds. Why should Romanists go to so much trouble to relieve suffering in Protestant countries while their religion produces the same sorts of suffering in their own countries?

Not all Catholics accept the diabolical doctrines of the Church. Shall we therefore refuse to find out what those doctrines are? But somebody is responsible for the hellish doctrines and practices of that Church. By the grace of God we shall find out just what the priests have to do with it all.

Besides the above, there are certain important matters which Protestants ought to consider: (1) The Mission Boards of all Protestant Churches are now committed to the policy of working among Catholics. (2) It is wrong for Protestants not to know the essentials of a religion which is all around them and which ignores their right to be called Christian. (3) The leaders of Romanism have deliberately kept back from us the most important teachings of their religion. (4) The Romish clergy appeal to our sense of fair play, while they refuse to play fair. They call us bigots, while they pretend that there is no salvation outside of the Catholic Church. They use brutal force to prevent us in our Christian work among Catholics while they busy themselves making proselytes from Protestantism. They clamor for liberty of worship while they refuse it to Protestants wherever it can be done without "scandal." They claim the right to celebrate matrimony while they slander as adulterous those converted Catholics who marry without the priest.

Shall we take the position that the published standards of Romanism do not represent the Church, or that Catholicism is whatever a given Catholic happens to believe? Admitting the genuineness of all the iniquities which are taught and sanctioned by Catholic theologians, censored and recommended by the proper authorities, and set forth by Catholic publishing houses or by those houses which have been selected by the authorities for that purpose, shall we conclude that the printed doctrines have no influence on the membership? Why do Romish popes, cardinals, bishops, etc., sanction printed moral filth if it is not that it may be practiced? Do they regard it as a sort of ornament to the sublime doctrines of the Trinity, of angelology, etc.? Must they have mud in order that their pearls may shine the brighter? Nay, verily; out of the abundance of the heart the mouth speaketh. "Doth the fountain send forth

from the same opening sweet water and bitter?"
The infinite varieties of sin and crime duly authorized
in detail by the highest standards of Romanism completely nullify whatever moral platitudes there are to
to be found in the books put out for popular con-
sumption.

In "Roman Catholicism Analyzed" I gave a
bird's-eye view of Romanism from the viewpoint
of a citizen of a democratic government. In "Papal
Paganism" I undertake to examine the nature of
Romanism as a religion among the various non-
Christian religions of the world.

The twentieth century is preëminently the period
in which Christianity must and will define her principles. The world is clamoring for a religion with an
unspotted system of ethics, a code on which all nations can unite. The human race is hungry for such
a knowledge of God as will satisfy the deepest long-
ings of the heart. The efforts now being made to
establish international peace indicate a general desire for a philosophy which can become universal.

If Romanism is a branch of the Christian religion,
as many writers believe it to be, the fact should be
demonstrated; if it is not, it should be made plain.
We are tired of camouflage. Catholic priests
craftily conceal the officially accepted principles of
the system and flatly deny the intrinsic perfidy of
their religion. These Jesuitical "spiritual guides"
even pretend that their "Mother Church" is
slandered when quotation after quotation from their
own highest authorities is given to show the utter
baseness of genuine Romish moral theology.

Only a heathen religion could be the mother of such

2

a vile brood as is hidden under the skirts of Romish theology. But no other form of paganism has ever been capable of such marvelous deceit. Some Protestant ministers now and then bow the knee before the great beast.

On the essentials Romanism never changes. But what are the essentials? Certainly her code of morals, her philosophy of civil government, and her notions as to God and the means of grace which are supposed to save from sin are essentials. That Romish theologians have held and disseminated, and do hold and disseminate immoral, treasonable, and superstitious doctrines, in the name and with the full authority of the Church, is certain. That these doctrines are inherent in the system may be tested by an endeavor to get a Romanist to denounce any one of them publicly.

The reader should consult the articles on "Jesuits," "Casuistry," "Liguori," and "Inquisition," in the Encyclopedia Britannica (Ninth edition), also the article on "Ultramontanism" in the Eleventh edition. If any one doubts that the essential wickedness of Romanism is entirely modern, and not merely medieval, he would do well to read "Religious Liberty in South America," by John Lee, 1907.

For the sake of brevity I frequently refer the reader to documents and arguments in my former work, "Roman Catholicism Analyzed," and to the Spanish edition of it, *"Analisis del Romanismo."* The latter contains some excellent documents not in the former.

Various personal friends have given important suggestions, for which I am profoundly grateful.

Two of these critics have been invaluable. Rev. Sidney McHenry Bedford, A.M., B.D., pastor of the First Christian Church of Roswell, N. Mex., has been most unsparing in his criticisms; these have been of immense benefit. Rev. M. C. Wilcox, Ph.D., Mount Vernon, Iowa, a ripe scholar, an authority on Comparative Religion, and twenty-five years a missionary in China, has corrected the MS. with great care. THE AUTHOR.

PART I

THE NATURE, ORIGIN, ENLARGEMENT, AND EVOLUTION OF ROMANISM

(21)

CHAPTER I

THE PAGAN NATURE OF ROMANISM

DURING the past fifty years literally thousands of scientists, missionaries, travelers, business men, and theologians have devoted their best energies to the investigation of the religions of the world.

Never before has such a wealth of material been brought before us. No one man could possibly go over all the field and secure first-hand information as to the infinite forms of religion among men. At the very beginning hundreds of strange languages would block his path. Then would follow peculiar prejudices, unfathomable ignorance, fierce passions, vague traditions. These obstacles are accentuated by the natural secretiveness of tribes and peoples who recognize no obligations to make known to strangers their most intimate beliefs.

In addition to all these difficulties we must add that the origins of religions run far back into history where the records are often very meager. Still further back there were primitive practices and ideas which can be traced only in the most superficial way; but here and there are to be found certain imperishable prehistoric remains.

Despite all this, years of research have yielded up the lore of inscriptions among tombs and buried cities, while contemporary savage tribes have become tractable, and scholars have delved into such higher faiths as Buddhism, Mohammedanism, Brahmanism, etc.

After the facts thus gained have been brought together philosophers have collated and, as far as possible, organized them into systems. Underlying the strange and weird phenomena of a great multiplicity of cults a remarkable bond of union has been discovered. This union constitutes the basis of the comparatively new science of Comparative Religion. Christianity, as well as all non-Christian faiths, is included in these investigations. Romanism can be no exception to the rule. In the light of Comparative Religion the Catholic system cannot be classed as Christian; it is profoundly pagan.

To say that Romanism is pagan is not to accuse her of something; it is merely to state a fact. Pagan religions have all had their place; it would be unfair to brand all of them as wholly evil. They are not inventions of the devil as theologians once claimed they were. The religious instinct has ever moved men and tribes to seek the cause and purpose of those invisible and mysterious forces which lay back of all phenomena, and to bring themselves into some sort of harmony with the First Cause or the primary causes or the mysterious governing beings.

All forms of idolatry, superstition, magic, and priestcraft seem to be capable of transformation into higher forms. Priests may give way to prophets, ministers, teachers, and physicians. Idolatry may permit a higher philosophy leading to monotheism; taboo may lead up to real reverence for God and for the majesty of law; fetishism may be dissolved by the light of a personal God. All this has taken place in historical times.

While there have been improvement and evolution among the non-Christian cults, there is no case on record where any of them ever developed into Christianity. The religion of Christ finds in man a religious instinct, but Jesus speaks with an authority which will brook no compromise. The best that other religions can do is to direct the attention of their followers toward an absolute religion revealed by a Supreme Being. No cult willingly surrenders to another; much less do the non-Christian religions turn over their disciples, bag and baggage, to the Christian faith. Yet there is often a desire to know what Christianity has to offer to the world.

But the Catholic religion is peculiar in that it is the only form of paganism which has perniciously continued with all of its original elements of natural religion. Instead of modifying and softening its heathenism the Catholic religion has become more rigid and more desperate in its long fight against Christianity. There is no priesthood in the world which claims such blasphemous authority. There has never been a system of idolatry as thoroughly persistent and powerful as is the idolatry of Rome. The magic which Romish theologians have worked into the very fiber of their seven sacraments is the most daring and the most sacrilegious of all heathen magic. Romish superstitions are so defended and dignified by solemn doctors of the law that the faithful hug them to their bosoms with blind and deathless tenacity.

While the Catholic religion was at its height—*i. e.,*

in the thirteenth and fourteenth centuries—it was unquestionably more wicked and bloody than in the fourth century, but it does not follow that it was essentially different. We must grant the Romish contention that *from its beginning* there has been nothing introduced into Romanism which was *radically new*. All that the popes and councils of the Dark Ages, or before or since, have declared with full authority was *implicit* in the early Roman Catholic Church and those doctors only made it *explicit*. Moreover, all that was once *implicit*, and which afterwards became *explicit*, is always and everywhere *essential*. Now, since a given doctrine or teaching has been authoritatively declared, it becomes heresy for any one to reject it.

In order for us to know clearly what was in Romanism at the beginning of her career it is only necessary to find out what was specifically declared during the height of her prosperity. We know what was implicit in the acorn only when we study the full-grown oak. It is logical to conclude that whatever was inherent in Romanism during her period of glory was inherent in her at the very beginning of her history. What do we find in Romanism as vital to her existence during the time of her greatest influence? Idolatry and, along with that, a future life determined by favoritism, and the unseen world largely controlled by thaumaturgy, a vague deposit of revelation, a luxuriant growth of magical formulæ, spurious miracles and degrading superstitions, an almost omnipotent priesthood, the utter subjection of morals to ecclesiastical authority, and civil governments gasping for breath. These are the ubiquitous seven elements which always form the warp and woof of paganism and Romanism. Celibacy, auricular confession, papal infallibility, etc., were only developments of priestly power.

We must admit that the systematic immoral casuistry developed by the Jesuits in the sixteenth century was not worked out and stated clearly in detail in the fourth century; it was only "implicit" at that early period. If ritual was so important in the fourth century that those who regarded morals as superior to ceremonies were *officially* adjudged as worthy of death, then the *official* religion was immoral; if immoral, it was anti-Christian. A practical test of paganism is this: Is it primarily ceremonial or sacerdotal in a way which makes morality always secondary in case of conflict between rites and ethics? If Romanism, on examination, proves to be guilty of placing priestly authority above morality, then it is pagan. If she *began* that way, then she *began pagan*.

It is true that the Christianity of the first, second, third, and most of the fourth century contained a considerable element of paganism. What, then, is the radical difference between the primitive form of Christianity with a few heathen notions and practices, and the Roman Catholic religion when it began to play the rôle of a Christian religion? It is simply the temporal punishment of dissenters, usually culminating in the death penalty for heresy.

Virtually all religions have certain things in common: Life after death, future rewards and punishments, a personal supreme God (this is a vague belief lying in the background of practically all religions), some phases of the moral code, a father god, the incarnation of God, the sacrificial death of gods, a remarkable number of sacred days, the reverent treatment of corpses, the religious character of marriage, divine authority in human government.

But those elements which differentiate Christianity from all other religions stand as an ideal sheer above even the table-lands of the highest non-Christian systems. These are seen in the climaxes of the Sermon on the Mount; as, "Blessed are the peacemakers, for they shall be called the children of God," "Let your light so shine before men, that they may see your good works, and glorify your Father which is in heaven"; "Be ye therefore perfect, even as your Father in heaven is perfect"; "Seek ye first the kingdom of God, and his righteousness; and all these things shall be added unto you"; "All things whatsoever ye would that men should do to you, do ye even so to them: for this is the law and the prophets"; "Thy will be done in earth, as in heaven." These highest goals cannot descend from their unique place; their prophets and disciples must ever labor toward their realization for themselves and for mankind. Rising still above those clear principles stands the author of them, giving us his personal power and presence.

Virtually all religions are hoary with age. Changes and combinations are to be found in all faiths except that of the Hebrew and Christian Scriptures. The Roman Catholic religion is no exception to the general rule.

Christianity is only an incident in the Roman Catholic (Holy Catholic) Church. The loss of arms, legs, and eyes, should one survive it, would not change one's identity. But if we could imagine the loss of heart, brain, liver, lungs, bones, alimentary canal, and nerves, and the replacement of all these, we should be forced to conclude that the product would be a new and different person. The essential seven elements of heathenism and Romanism which we shall examine in detail a little later—to wit, a deficient chief deity, the other world and the future life governed by priests, a precarious deposit of revelation, magical ceremonies, a wonder-working priesthood, a bad moral code, and union of Church and State, which has usually resulted in the killing of heretics—constitute the whole essence of a non-Christian religion. An examination of the genesis and various stages of development of Romanism will reveal the fact that after several centuries of struggle for the purpose of ejecting the body of Christian doctrine which she swallowed and never was able to assimilate, that Church merely reasserted all her original pagan principles and then continued on her way precisely as she did before Christ was ever heard of. Romanism is not a crippled form of Christianity; it is simply the religion of Italy with the same heart, brain, liver, lungs, bones, alimentary canal, and nerves, all taking the name and endeavoring to take the form of the religion which it displaced. If we cared to press the analogy, we might say that Romanism has always had a degenerate heart, a distorted brain, a fatty liver, an omnivorous alimentary canal (we might even say, carnivorous), and a network of nerves which reaches through the confessional to the furthermost extremity of her body politic. As to her lungs, she has always breathed in the air of pagan sentiment, while her bones stand unchangeably in the strength of ancient heathen power.

The line of cleavage between all forms of paganism and Christianity is this: Does a given religion claim the right to punish or even kill those who would insist on the superiority of morality to rites and ceremonies? Virtually all pagan religions make that claim; Christianity does not. The underlying reason for this difference is the two ideas of God or the gods as held by these respective systems. The gods of paganism are narrow, capricious, weak, cruel, ignorant, and pompous. They must have their pound of flesh. The sinner must pay for his sins by penance; likewise he may pay for his salvation, and a little more, by superabundant works. If mercy is shown, it must be done according to the royal proceedings of an Oriental monarch or a savage chief. Pagan deities are limited; they must have representatives, and it is not important that these agents be upright; they must simply be loyal to their godlings. Favoritism is one of the prime evils of pagan cults; moral character is neither a means nor a goal among Romanists or pagans. Precise forms of belief must be subscribed to; adherence to the tribal religion must be unquestioned; exact performance of prescribed ritual must be carried out, and a priesthood with magical powers is essential. Magic—that is, the mysterious powers of ceremonies and of the priest to work wonders in the natural and spiritual world—is the beginning point of non-Christian cults.

All Catholic and almost all Protestant theologians hold that the Roman Catholic religion is nineteen centuries old. I do not hesitate to differ squarely from all of those who believe that. According to all rules of evidence and logic Romanism is at least twenty-five hundred years old.

SEVEN VITAL ELEMENTS IN ALL RELIGIONS

1. There must be a *god or gods* as the basis of any religion; without a deity or several deities there can be no religion. The god or gods may have a very feeble personality; devotees may have only a vague idea of the nature of that which they worship, but there must be some sort of force or intelligence which is regarded as being in one or more ways superior to the worshiper.

2. The question of *the other world and the future life* demands consideration. It is partly or mainly the dread of death and the mysterious other world that impels men to some sort of religion. The notion of a future life may be very faint. Herbert Spencer, in tracing the evolution of religion, made its beginning depend upon the savage belief in the "other self." He held that as long as the living dreamed of the dead it was because the other self, which did not die, was supposed to be still in existence. The higher religions have a much more prolonged life after death than do the primitive cults. But all religions have some sort of a theory of the future life.

3. Any religion has a sort of *deposit of revelation;* this may be in the form of literature or it may be merely held in the minds of the faithful and transmitted from generation to generation.

4. All cults have certain *methods of approach to deity*. It must be by thought and sentiment; these may be highly developed or sentiment may almost

exclude thinking, but there is always some sort of ratiocination. In the exercise and cultivation of sentiment and thought forms must be used; they may include incantations, but there is always the idea of prayer and usually song and music. Fasts and feasts, pilgrimages, the sacrificial meal, penance, etc., are usually parts of the system which is supposed to bring the devotee into harmony with the gods.

5. *An agency* is everywhere present as an indispensable part of a cult. It might be argued that such was not necessary, but facts prove otherwise. This agency may be in the main priestly, or it may be primarily of the order of teaching; in all cases there is some teaching.

6. *Morality must occupy a place in all religions;* it may be placed very high in the cult or it may occupy an insignificant position. No tribe or people would be satisfied if their religion utterly ignored the question of morals.

7. It is inevitable that a religion should have a *philosophy of civil government.* Constant contact with the State makes it necessary that a theory be developed as to the right relations which should exist between the religion and the government or governments with which it has to do.

CHRISTIANITY AND THE SEVEN VITAL ELEMENTS OF RELIGION

1. The Christian religion has *only one God;* he may be called the Most High, or the Supreme Being, or the Heavenly Father, or God Almighty, or Jehovah; but whatever he is called he brooks no rival. The doctrine of the Trinity does not imply tritheism;

there are not three gods. We have found out the
nature of God through the life, teaching, death, resurrection, and ever-growing influence of Jesus Christ.
He does not contradict the highest conception of a
just, merciful, wise, and powerful God. The power
he exercised while on earth was worthy of the Almighty; it dealt specifically with man, his sin and
salvation. The name of Jesus has had a marvelous
charm to win and inspire and instruct men all through
the centuries.

Monotheism is essential in the cultivation of
morality because it centers responsibility in one
authority. Without the idea of one God a nation can
have no real intelligent unity. Whatever peace there
may be established under a multiplicity of gods, it is
based on the power and cunning of the few (priests,
kings, or chiefs) who hold the masses in their control.
No polytheistic nation can be permanent, because
there is in the human heart an innate thirst for
justice and truth. The masses will ever be ready to
rise in rebellion as long as there are gods many and
lords many to direct the consciences of men in diverse
ways.

2. *Christianity teaches that we shall all live eternally*
after death and that our destiny is settled by the love
and mercy of God and our faith and obedience to
him as his children. The Christian religion shows no
favoritism. "God is no respecter of persons: but in
every nation he that feareth him, and worketh righteousness, is accepted with him." Christianity does
not people the other world with grinning devils who
are ready to carry off heretics to the shades of the
dead unless they repent of their struggles for freedom

3

and appeal to the holy Virgin or to some lesser saint
or else flourish some fetish in the face of the enemy
of souls.

3. *The deposit of revelation is, according to Christianity, the sixty-six books of the Bible as it was received in the three or four first centuries of the Christian
era.* No other revelation is needed to make a man
thoroughly "furnished unto every good work."
Man's memory is too treacherous to be depended
upon accurately to conserve and transmit God's
revealed truths to mankind; besides, Bible Christians
are, as a matter of fact, equipped for right living.

4. *Christianity uses song, prayer, the symbolic
sacrificial meal, the simple rite of baptism, the sermon,
meditation, and especially the sacred day of rest and
worship, as means of grace.* Sentiment is cultivated,
but it does not overshadow reason. The progress of
Christian nations in science, invention, discovery,
the use of medicine, the beneficent functions of
government and of the Christian Churches, demon-
strates that Christianity is a religion of thought as
well as of heart experience.

Christianity, among all the religions of the world,
allows the most adverse criticism of its doctrines and
practices. A real Christian cannot be a fanatic without surrendering his religious philosophy. He must
think and let think if he is truly to represent the
Nazarene.

5. *The agency whose life work it is to represent
Christianity is composed of men whose first principle
must be personal righteousness and whose efficiency
depends on the exercise of the right kind of influence.
A Christian minister is a preacher of righteousness*

rather than a mere administrator of sacraments. Paul thanked God that he was not sent to baptize, but to preach the gospel. A preacher is a prophet in the sense that he "speaketh unto men to edification, and exhortation, and comfort." It is the business of Christian leaders to understand the trend of their times, to discern the dangers threatening the people, to guide individuals and nations in the realm of morals and religion.

6. *In the Christian religion moral character is supreme.* Back of that is the impulse to glorify God and enjoy his love, but this does not conflict with the ethical life. On the contrary, it nourishes it. A Christian seeks first the kingdom of God and his righteousness. The righteousness of God goes far beyond the demands of men. It opposes evil and restores the delinquent, whereas the righteousness of man merely punishes the wrongdoer, but is unable to work a change of heart or reformation. The code of morals taught and practiced by Jesus Christ is without a parallel in any age or race. And this is the system of righteousness which Christians undertake to follow and propagate. It has in it the note of universality on the principle of influence, persuasion, and instruction. It is the duty of Christians to inculcate the Master's system of morality in the whole world.

7. *Christianity does not depart from its Founder by endeavoring to control civil government.* As citizens, Christians use their influence to make governments better, but they do not feel called upon to suppress those of another faith by the use of temporal power. Freedom under the law is the same now in the minds

and practice of Christians as it was in the method and teaching of Jesus and the apostles. The followers of Christ are to be the light of the world and the salt of the earth—that is, they are to teach and to exercise a good influence.

WHAT IS PAGANISM?

Paganism is that form of religion in which man-created gods, usually represented by images, preside over the affairs of the world, especially the future and the unseen, giving their revelations, accompanied by magical formulæ, to an unscrupulous priesthood who pay scant attention to morality and seek by means of civil law and spiritual threats to impose their entire system on dissenters.

THE FOUR SO-CALLED NOTES OF THE CATHOLIC CHURCH

Romish theologians claim that their Church is founded on four principles—to wit, Unity, Sanctity, Catholicity, and Apostolicity.

We not only grant, but we contend, that the Catholic Church has unity in all parts of the world and in all the past. Wherever there is an apparent inconsistency, it is due to a misunderstanding. For instance, in a vigorous Protestant country the Church does not seem to believe it the duty of the Catholic Church to dominate civil government, because she does not try to practice temporal control, or at least she does not succeed in practicing it. Catholics in Protestant countries may not generally practice the doctrine of theft (secret compensation) or the doctrine of gambling, but we have no right to infer from

that that the Church has changed; it is only that
some of the members differ from the tenets of their
own religion. If Catholics seem not to "condemn,
reject, and anathematize" those Protestant doctrines
and practices which are contrary to the Catholic
doctrines, it is only because they have been somewhat
Protestantized. No Catholic has the right to believe
in liberty of worship for Protestants as a principle;
if a Catholic really believes that, it is because he has
to that extent become a heretic.

Was there ever a time when the Roman Catholic
religion did not teach what it does to-day? Yes; but
it did not teach very many things which may be regarded as contradictory to its present-day doctrine.
Take papal infallibility, for instance. The Church
has always believed that there was some sort of
infallibility lying around loose, but just where it was
located no one knew until 1870. That was a long
time to wait for so important a matter to be settled,
but the uncertainty of the thing gave large scope to
priestly authority and served thereby an important
purpose. Papal supremacy in matters of discipline
was inherent all through the ages; the problem was
how to force it on the lower clergy and on the civil
governments. It was present in its germ centuries
before Christ.

Catholicity is the conceit that the Church will become universal some time. We need not be concerned about that as long as we believe in the goodness of God and in the universal spread of Christianity.

The Romish claim to apostolicity is absurd. One
has only to glance at the fundamentals of Romanism

to see that they are not even hinted at in the writings of the apostles. There is no sign that Peter or Paul ever carried around relics under their clothes, or that they sneaked into confessional boxes and tried to get the women to come and tell them a lot of things their husbands were not to know about, or that they ever fell down before images of the Virgin or the saints.

The whole Romish system stands or falls with its claim to sanctity or holiness. If that Church is peculiarly holy in her doctrines or her fruits, we shall have to admit that she is apostolic and universal.

The doctrines of Romanism are not only unholy, but positively demoralizing. Some of the so-called saints of Catholicism were incarnate devils; for instance, the inquisitorial saints. But one of the most eminent saints of the whole pantheon—that is, Alphonso Maria de Liguori—was the most corrupt teacher in the realm of morals that ever disgraced the world. There have been more brazen teachers of iniquity, but Liguori is the most demoralizing because he was so profoundly hypocritical; he has been able to lead astray millions upon millions, whereas other unscrupulous men have corrupted only their thousands.

THE EARMARKS OF PAGANISM, AND THEREFORE OF ROMANISM

The *basis* of heathenism is *laziness*, manual labor being regarded as beneath the dignity of the higher classes. The thought that man is to conquer the earth does not enter the head of an ordinary pagan; he is a stranger to science and to the Christian's hope of victory over nature. Having little idea of a sacred rest day, work is not sacred and there is little joy in labor. Romanists placed Sunday on a level with or a little below saints' days. Their catechisms in Romish countries say, "Remember to sanctify the feasts," instead of "Remember the Sabbath day, to keep it holy." Romanism sanctions Sabbath desecration. Here is the law:

What work is permitted on Sunday? Every so-called liberal work, such as reading, writing, teaching, *drawing, and painting*. Common works; such, for example, as *traveling, hunting, and fishing*. . . . So also, the *buying or selling houses, horses*, etc., provided that these transactions take place between private individuals. The buying and selling of victuals, etc., in public stores. . . . What are the causes that justify servile work on Sunday? Dispensation, *custom*.[1]

Surrender of private judgment, leaving the work of Bible study and the whole question of morals to those who have laid on them the magical hands of those predecessors who are in holy orders, develops indolence. Granting infallibility to the pope also promotes intellectual and spiritual laziness.

The results of this scheme are seen in the poverty of both Catholic and heathen countries. This loathing for work is not necessarily in the blood; it comes from lack of hopefulness, the caste system, dependence on the priest, illiteracy, and the artificial authority of the theologians to allow or forbid.

1. *A variety of gods; especially a goddess*. Pagans admit that they worship all sorts of male and female gods. Catholics do render the sort of obedience to their popes, their saints, and to Mary that is not allowable to any one except to gods. In rank Catholic countries, where the devotees are not ashamed to

---

[1] "Manual of Christian Doctrine."

practice their religion in all its naked and hideous
glory, images, relics, charms, shrines, and statues
abound to a most detestable degree. *The so-called
religious loyalty to the pope* as against the plain
maxims of morality and the reasonable demands of
patriotism is a ubiquitous distinction of all true
Catholics.

2. *Ungrounded fears of the unseen world and of the
future beyond the grave* is a universal mark of heathenism. Of course there are so-called Catholics, thousands and perhaps millions of them, who do not
believe in the Catholic purgatory. The thoughtful
men among them are usually skeptical as to the high
temperature of purgatory and hell. The better element among Catholics realize the absurdity of a hell
for those who send their children to a public school,
who regularly attend Protestant meetings, who read
the Bible without Catholic notes and translations, or
who refuse to commit perjury in order to denounce
heretics, who refuse to answer the vile questions pro-
pounded by priests, or who believe in liberty of worship for Protestants. But the better element in the
Catholic Church cannot properly be classed with
genuine Romanists.

If the masses of Romanists throughout the world
should suddenly reject the Catholic doctrine of sin
and hell and purgatory, it would so deplete the treas-
ury of Rome that the Church would have to go beg-
ging. The vicious doctrine of hell and purgatory
enables the priests to frighten their people into filling
the coffers of the ungodly clergy.

But that is also the underlying power of all pagan
religions. Priests must be supported; people will not

willingly support them, for they do not respect them; it follows that the people must be taught to believe that these men are indispensable to save them from the wrath of the deities. Faithful Catholics usually accept the offices of the priests just as they would the work of the garbage man; not because they really respect or believe in the man, but because they have a sort of feeling (not a belief) that there may be a set of gods who will call them to account after death, for their neglect of priestly conditions of salvation.

Unfortunately this fear of the unseen world is not the fear of sin, or its inevitable consequences, but fear of the gods and the priests. The Catholic dread of purgatory, hell, and *limbus infantum* is absolutely pagan. It is not sin that sends them to those horrible places, but such trivial matters as a refusal to fast, carelessness in saying the canonical hours, or heedlessness during prayers, or the accident of not being baptized in infancy. Real sins, especially lying and perjury, if done for the glory of the Church, are not only excused, but are classified as virtues.

3. *Neither Romanists nor Buddhists give much attention to the study of their deposit of revelation; in each case it is regarded as the special task of the priests.* The Romish clergy have purposely mixed a great mass of rubbish with their Bible in order to make it impossible for the ordinary member of the Church to get true guidance from the precepts of his own religion. It is only necessary to reflect that in genuine Catholic countries the people do not have the Bible. It is only where Protestantism forces it on the priests that Catholics have an easy way to get Catholic Bibles.

All pagans regard their priests as belonging to a specially high caste who have the magical power of understanding the laws of the gods. If there were a consistent moral code given by one god, it would not be so complicated as to require specialists to the exclusion of the common people. In the realm of reason and science specialists do not prohibit the laity from learning all they can or from using their own judgment in the understanding of facts and principles. In the religious sphere heathen and Romanists regard the laws as so far above reason and science that there must be men magically equipped in order to understand them. If the morality of Romanism were pure and right, the laity could understand it without such juggling.

4. *Magic is found everywhere among genuine Catholics just as truly as among African savages.* The sign of the cross is recommended for the purpose of driving away devils who are supposed to be capable of doing bodily harm. That is just as far from Christianity as is any savage idea of charms and fetishes. This shows itself in various ways.

Slavery to passion is a concomitant of magic and a universal element of heathenism. Pagans are not generally guided by reason; they seldom reflect before they act. Revenge, hate, and blind fanaticism pervade Romanism. It was the pagan spirit which moved the Jews to clamor for the death of Jesus, crying, "Crucify him; crucify him." It is precisely the same anti-Christian animus which inspires Catholic mobs to attack lecturers who expose the wickedness of Romanism. In Paul's day the heathen cried, "Great is Diana of the Ephesians;" in our day

Romanists echo back, "Great is the Pontiff of the Romans." With a multitude of gods and a great goddess, with magic and not reason as the basis of their thinking, with a group of black-robed priests to fill them with venom, the ancient and the modern Romans raise the same howl against a spiritual religion because it threatens to wrench the victims of priestcraft from the grasp of those who hate Jesus Christ and the moral code which he gave to the world.

Refusal to bear responsibility and the disposition to take advantage of the diligence of neighbors is a double evil of paganism. It is a direct result of the separation between cause and effect. The Romish Church has always had the habit of shirking responsibility for her own acts. The established custom that a priest must not shed blood is the blackest hypocrisy. It is the duty of the priesthood to require the civil government to imprison and kill, but their hands must be washed of it as Pilate washed his hands of the blood of Jesus Christ. During all the weary centuries when the Catholic Church had men tortured and killed for their faithfulness and loyalty to conviction, it was her delight to force the "secular power" to do her brutal work.

When the Spanish Inquisition was at its height it was the Romish Church that trumped up and instigated every charge; but since the Inquisition has become odious in the light of Protestant freedom, according to her long-established pagan practice, she files a disclaimer, laying all the blame on the over-zealous Spaniards. They say the Inquisition was milder in Italy. Well, if they had chloroformed their

victims when they tortured them, we might catch a
gleam of their "tender mercies," but history records
no case of anæsthesia to soften the Satanic cruelties of
even the Italian Inquisition. The Brief of Julius II.
shows that it was the pope who forced the secular
arm to persecute heretics.[2]

For four centuries the duly authorized priests of
Rome—sent from Catholic Spain and Italy—have
debauched the peoples of Latin America. Now, after
this exploitation, the Church complains that the
blood is bad and that neither Holy Mother Church nor
anybody else could elevate the natives of America.
The results of Protestant mission work in Latin
America prove that this charge is false. The Scripture says that the gospel is "the power of God unto
salvation to every one that believeth." And thousands of competent witnesses testify that it holds true
in every Latin-American nation.

In the Catholic doctrines which sanction theft,
under the euphonious name of "secret compensation," and fraud in the matter of short weights and
measures, the whole responsibility is thrown on the
stingy employer, in the first instance, and oppressive
big merchants in the second.

As pagan Rome took advantage of the industry of
her subject tribes, so modern Romanism would fain
claim the credit for the prosperity of Protestant America. With the baldest hypocrisy Lord Baltimore, with
his liberal laws for Maryland, is cited as a humble
follower of the Lamb on the Tiber. Had the Bull of
Boniface VIII. been applied to Lord Baltimore, his
tolerant statutes would have been nullified before the

---

[2] "Roman Catholicism Analyzed," pp. 246, 248.

ink was dry. His main purpose was to secure good colonists and he knew that the Protestants were among the best and most industrious.

The natural effect of magic is to sever the connection between cause and effect. It is especially inimical to science and morals. A genuine Catholic will not reason about his so-called faith, nor will he examine its iniquitous aspects. Romanists seem to be unable to understand the logical consequences of their own beliefs, or, rather, their non-belief. Irish Catholics, for instance, have continually blamed England and the English for the Irish troubles; but now that they have a free hand to settle their own difficulties with a minimum of outside interference, they cannot agree with each other. It is amusing how Romish theologians try to evade responsibility for the Inquisition. One single fact is enough to convince any reasonable man that Rome is still guilty of the premeditated murder and high-handed robbery practiced by popes, bishops, and their faithful followers in the middle ages and for some time afterwards; to wit, the worship of canonized Inquisitors.

This same effect of magic in breaking the connection between cause and effect in the moral realm is seen in the unblushing assertions that the clean character of some good men in the Catholic Church is due to the religious and moral teaching of that Church. The high moral character of any Catholic comes either from his contact with Protestants or from the private teaching of his upright father and mother, in spite of the diabolical doctrines of his own religion. Catholics even go so far as to claim at least some of the credit for the greatness of the government of the United States. Had this government been Catholic, there would be no public worship by any of the Protestant Churches; we would be now under the rule of the liquor traffic, we would have had gambling and lotteries all over the country, we would have the almost universal practice of "secret compensation"—that is, theft; we would have no public schools except as they were under the control of the priests. All that would mean fifty per cent illiteracy of the people, degradation on account of drunkenness and gambling, and instability because of "secret compensation."

Incantations, repetitions of long prayers, fasts, pilgrimages to shrines and to Rome, and penance are just as common among Catholics as among pagans.

5. *Abject submission to a priesthood* and the fanaticism resulting from such fettered thinking and conduct are almost as common among real Romanists as they are among South Sea Islanders. It is the constant task of Catholic priests to deceive those whom they cannot degrade and to debauch those who do not resent priestly perfidy. Mobs for the defense of the iniquitous doctrines and practices of Romanism prove that system to be purely pagan.

6. *The exalted moral code of Jesus Christ is a rock of offense for Catholic and pagan priests.* The system of ethics which Jesus gave us would weaken the magical hold of the priestly class on their devotees; it would rouse the faithful to independent thinking; it would pour ice water on their so-called zeal for the "Faith." A high moral code would make a priesthood unnecessary, for the business of the priest is to substitute claptrap for character, magic for

morals, sacraments for sanctity, and flummery for faith.

Those who have lived in the midst of solid blocks of Catholics know full well how tricky they are with regard to the truth and how their religion is generally regarded as something apart from their moral life. This is the same deadly defect that is found among pagans. It is not an accident that gambling, bull-fighting, and drinking are in control in Spain, where Romanism revels in her pristine glory and rottenness.

7. *All Catholics and all pagans are known by their supercilious attitude toward civil government.* When I say *"all* Catholics" I do not include those who are so far Protestantized as to accept the heretical doctrine of the separation of Church and State and the various forms of freedom which attend that doctrine; such are not genuine Catholics, no matter how strongly they may profess Church loyalty.

THE HEART OF ROMANISM AS IT IS SEEN IN THE CREED OF PIUS IV.

By dissecting the Creed of Pius IV. and rearranging the articles under the classification of Catholic principles which we have already made, we may demonstrate that Romanism is essentially pagan.

1. *The gods.* "I most firmly assert that the images of Christ, of the Mother of God, ever Virgin, and also of other saints, ought to be had and retained, and that due honor and veneration are to be given them." In the article preceding the devotee says that he steadfastly holds "that the saints reigning together with Christ are to be honored and invocated, and that they offer prayers to God for us."

2. *The future life a matter of favoritism.* "I stead-fastly hold that there is a Purgatory, and that the souls therein detained are helped by the suffrages of the faithful." Again, "I also affirm that the power of granting indulgences was left by Christ in the Church, and that the use of them is most wholesome to Christian people."

3. *A deposit of revelation has been left in the hands of the priests in such a way as to make it easy for them to exploit the people and keep them in ignorance.* "I most steadfastly admit and embrace the Apostolical and Ecclesiastical Traditions, and all other observances and constitutions of the same Church."

"I also admit the Holy Scriptures, according to that sense which our holy Mother the Church has held, and does hold, to which it belongs to judge of the true sense and interpretation of the Scriptures; neither will I ever take and interpret them otherwise than according to the unanimous consent of the Fathers."

4. *Magic.* "I also profess that there are truly and properly seven Sacraments of the New Law, instituted by Jesus Christ our Lord, and necessary for the salvation of mankind, although not all of them necessary for every one—namely, Baptism, Confirmation, the Eucharist, Penance, Extreme Unction, Order, and Matrimony; and that they confer grace; and that of these, Baptism, Confirmation, and Order cannot be repeated without the sin of sacrilege. I also receive and admit the approved ceremonies of the Catholic Church used in the solemn administration of the aforesaid Sacraments." It is not there stated that it is a mortal sin willfully to use other ceremonies for

those which have been duly prescribed by the pope, but that is Catholic law. The fatal doctrine that the sacraments confer grace is intrinsic in Romanism and it is pure magic. But the most abominable form of magic is found in the doctrine of the mass and of Transubstantiation. Note the following: "I profess likewise, that in the Mass there is offered to God a true, proper, and propitiatory Sacrifice for the living and the dead. And that in the most holy sacrifice of the Eucharist, there is truly, really, and substantially the Body and Blood, together with the soul and divinity of our Lord Jesus Christ, and there is made a conversion of the whole substance of the bread into the Body, and of the whole substance of the wine into the Blood, which conversion the Catholic Church calls Transubstantiation. I also confess that, under either kind alone, Christ is received whole and entire, and a true Sacrament."

The Catholic also must "steadfastly hold" that the relics of the saints "are to be held in veneration."

5. *A powerful and unscrupulous priesthood whose business it is to undermine morals by the use of magic, and to lead their membership into fanaticism and sin by exercising an ungodly authority over them.* "I embrace and receive all and every one of the things which have been defined and declared in the holy Council of Trent, concerning original sin and justification." The average Catholic knows as much about the decrees of the Council of Trent as does a Hottentot.

The blasphemy of submission to a priest is seen further in the following articles: "I acknowledge the

4

Holy, Catholic, Apostolic, Roman Church for the mother and mistress of all Churches, and I promise true obedience to the Bishop of Rome, Successor of Saint Peter, Prince of the Apostles, and Vicar of Jesus Christ. I likewise undoubtingly receive and profess all other things which the Sacred Canons and General Councils, and particularly the holy Council of Trent and the Ecumenical Vatican Council, have delivered, defined, and declared, and in particular, about the supremacy and infallible teaching of the Roman Pontiff. And I condemn, reject, and anathematize all things contrary thereto, and all heresies which the Church has condemned, rejected, and anathematized."

6. *The Creed of Pius IV. makes an inferior moral code inevitable.* In submitting to the priesthood, the theologians, the canons, and the decrees of the Catholic Church, and more especially to the supremacy and infallibility of the pope, the Catholic surrenders the right of private interpretation of Scripture; indeed he says as much when he agrees not to interpret the Bible except according to the unanimous consent of the fathers. The perfidy of this is not made perfectly clear in this creed; it is necessary to find out what the Church does teach through her accredited theologians. But the nerve of morality is cut when the Catholic agrees to understand the Scriptures "according to that sense which our holy Mother Church has held, and does hold." The condemnation and anathematization of everything contrary to Romanism, and this to be done without examining those things which are condemned, undermines the moral character of Catholics. As evidence of this see

the unblushing denials made by Catholics that they do curse Protestant doctrine.

7. *Antagonism to civil government* is unavoidable in the Catholic's abject submission to the supremacy of the pope, whom he calls the vicar of Jesus Christ. The sense in which the pope is Christ's vicar implies dominion over civil government in a way which no self-respecting nation in the world will allow.

CHAPTER II

THE PAGAN ORIGIN OF ROMANISM

MANY centuries before Christ there began two entirely different systems of religion; the one had its origin in Palestine, the other in Italy. Now, in the twentieth century A.D., we have the same two forms of religion, with no material change in either.

THE RELIGION WHICH WAS BORN IN PALESTINE

The Palestinian notion of religion is that there is only one God, with no inferior deities to help him and no images to represent small gods. The Jews first believed that there might be gods among the Gentiles; but that, at least for the Jews, there was only one God. Later in their history they reached the belief that all the gods of the Gentiles were vain.

Abraham left Ur of the Chaldees on account of his monotheistic belief. It was this principle that sustained him in his journeys. The Jews left Egypt on account of their belief in one God. The plagues sent on the Egyptians were so many volleys sent against their various gods. In all their desert wanderings the Israelites were inspired and organized by their faith in a good and wise God who was jealous of his honor and who would not admit a rival. The superiority of the twelve tribes of Israel to the idolatrous clans in Canaan was due to their doctrine of one God. It was this same ideal which gave to the best judges and kings their power and authority. When the

Northern ten tribes broke down in their monotheism
they went into captivity; a little more than a century
later, the two Southern tribes followed suit. Only on
condition that Judah had repented could she be permitted in the providence of God to return to the Holy
Land and take up her task again of giving to the
world this priceless treasure.

The Christian religion is the lineal descendant of
the Jewish. Our monotheism comes from that
source. It is set forth in the law of Moses, in the
book of Psalms, and in the writings of the prophets.
Our idea of a Messiah is traced by the New Testament writers back to the Hebrew notion. The superiority of morals over ceremonies comes from the
Israelites; the superiority of prophets over priests has
the same origin.

Jesus, the greatest interpreter of the Old Testament, states plainly that he came not to destroy the
law or the prophets, but to fulfill. Paul regards the
Christians as the spiritual children of Abraham.
Christians expect their religion to become universal
as truly as did the Jews that Judaism would be
world-wide, but in a much more practical way. The
Jews were to wait until the Gentiles came to them;
Christians believe it their duty and privilege to carry
their religion to the non-Christian world.

We may test the nature of the Palestinian religion
by the seven essentials of paganism.

1. *The Jews, as a nation or as a religious people,
never surrendered entirely to a régime of image-
worship*. Whenever they were guilty of such a practice it was regarded by the best Jews as backsliding.
All forms of image-worship were finally repudiated

by the entire Jewish race. The Jews had their great rabbis and they came perilously near to polytheism in their submission to some of those teachers; but the fact that there were rival schools of religion without an infallible priest, or rabbi, or ecclesiastical court made it impossible for them to elevate their theological teachers to the rank of small gods.

The Roman religion in the tenth century before Christ, in the twentieth century A.D., and during each century between these dates, has been wholly committed to image-worship and to the worship of small gods.

The burden of the prophets was the polytheism and idolatry of the people. It was called adulterous, abominable, filthy, treasonable, blasphemous, ruinous, degrading.

2. *Felicity in the future life, according to the Old Testament, was not to be determined by ritualistic observance*. Romanism and paganism make it almost impossible for dissenters to be happy in their heavens. The Hebrews always set forth a great and just God as the deity whom man should worship. Doctors of the law descended to quibbling, but they did not truly represent their religion. Romanists and pagans have ceremonialism ingrained in their cults so that no amount of comment can take it out. Jesus, the great expounder of true Judaism, said: "Many shall come from the east and west, and shall sit down with Abraham, and Isaac, and Jacob, in the kingdom of heaven. But the children of the kingdom shall be cast out into outer darkness." According to Jesus, it was the Good Samaritan, and not a Jewish priest or Levite, who was the model citizen in his kingdom.

3. *The deposit of revelation* among the Jews *was contained in the Old Testament as Protestants have it.* The Jews of Palestine never accepted the apocryphal books. Christians since the first centuries of the Christian era have uniformly accepted the Sacred Writings of the Jews as the background of the New Testament. Following the lead of the Jews, the Christians have granted liberty of interpretation to the laity. Neither Jews nor Christians have ever set up an infallible head with authority to interpret the Bible infallibly.

Both Roman priests and paganized Jewish Pharisees have made the Word of God of no effect by their tradition. In each case the mass of tradition was swept away by the Saviour as straws before a hurricane, by an appeal to the moral sense of the common people. This was done again by Luther and other Reformers.

But the task is more difficult when dealing with blind Romanists, for they have canonized theologians whose vagaries and iniquities are as binding as the laws of the Medes and Persians.

4. If there are to be found hints of *magic* among the ancient Hebrews, it can be explained as *a vestige of the heathenism* with which they were surrounded. Moreover, it did not become a vital part of the Jewish faith. The Masoretic method of comment on Scripture is no more an essential part of Judaism than is the allegorical method of interpretation a part of Protestantism. The Urim and Thummim was of so little consequence that we hardly know what it was; it certainly had little to do with Jewish religion or its interpretation.

The passion for righteousness embodied in the great prophets of Judah and Israel checkmated the tendency to heathen magic among the Jews.

There is nothing among the Jews comparable to the seven sacraments of the Catholics.

5. *While the Jews had priests, theirs was a religion of prophecy instead of magic.* The test of paganism in a priesthood is their claim to magical powers. If we were to find such power among the Jewish priests, it would be discovered in the definition of the Hebrew word *taher*, or rather t'h'r, which certainly does mean "to cleanse." It is used to signify the work of Almighty God—*e. g.*, Jeremiah xxxiii. 8, "I will cleanse them from all their iniquity"; also in Psalm lii. 2, Ezekiel xxxvi. 25, and various other passages. Now when the work of the priests in treating a case of leprosy is described, the identical word is used; see Leviticus xiii. and xiv. There the priest is said to *cleanse* the leper, when he really only *pronounces him clean.* So evident is this that the translators do not give the original, but simply say that he pronounces him clean.

It must be admitted on all hands that the Jewish religion grew and developed. At the coming of Jesus the priestly idea had largely given place to that of the study of the law. The destruction of Jerusalem was the deathblow to sacerdotalism; since then the priestly notion has practically vanished from among the Jews. Their rabbis expound the law and preach and lecture on modern problems, but sacrifice is practically nil since there is no temple.

The Hebrews never disgraced themselves with auricular confession. A confessional box among those people would have been as childish and ridiculous and sacrilegious as it would be among the Christians of Paul's day or the Christians of the twentieth century

We must not slander the heathen by charging all of them or any of them with such a polished engine of destruction as is the Romish confessional, yet we must admit that there is such a thing in embryo even among the most pagan peoples.

Romanists and many pagans claim that their priests have the power to make their gods out of dough or grain. The Jews were never so impious as that. The manufacture of gods out of flour is the height of pagan irreverence; it is also the acme of magic, for it violates all the authority of the five senses. It cannot be classed as miraculous, for all miracles depend upon their appeal to the senses, while this literal manufacture of deities demands the repudiation of the evidence brought by the physical senses.

The Romish system of indulgences is an extension of the heathen doctrine of penance and of priestly power; it is ultra-heathenism. Jewish priests were never so unscrupulous or so ungodly as that.

While the Jews were bigoted, they were never guilty of canonizing diabolical inquisitors; indeed they had nothing comparable to the Catholic inquisition. Jews have never thought it their duty to suppress or destroy all other religions.

There was divine authority for such a mild species of priesthood as the Jews had. Romanists shamelessly lay claim to Scriptural sanction for a sacerdotal caste which far outstrips the prerogatives of all Jewish and all heathen priesthoods. Besides, there is no provision made in the New Testament for any sort of a clergy with magical powers. It is only the deadly virus of heathenism in the Catholic cult which impels them to sport a pompous priesthood.

6. *The Jews have at times been guilty of a degrading casuistry,* but they have been preserved from ruin because they never had a system of sainthood presided over by an infallible head which fastened authorized iniquities on the membership. They had no power to nullify the plain teachings of Holy Writ. If their clergy had claimed such authority, they, like the Catholics, would have endeavored to prevent their people from reading the Bible.

Were there in Judaism such an authorized diabolical system of casuistry as there is in Romanism, it would be worthless as an instrument for the destruction of morals because they have no confessional box where it could be brought to bear upon individuals.

All heathen priests, and the Romish clergy in particular, make a peculiar pretense to knowledge on account of their magical power. The Jews never made the silly claim of infallibility for their high priest. This relieves them from another mark of paganism.

7. *The Jews never made statecraft primary in their religion.* That is an essential difference between them and all heathen. All pagans, Romanists in particular, demand a unique authority for their priesthood in the realm of civil government. The Jews endeavored theoretically to give considerable power to their priests; but in practice it was their prophets who rebuked and advised kings. It re-

quired several centuries for the Roman Catholic Church to secure the same recognition of the new head of the State—that is, the pope—which had been given to the emperors before the time of Theodosius. But the pagan claim never varied for a moment. Romanism with its new name (Roman Catholic Church) held that the head of both Church and State was the same man and that he had magical power to control the religious ceremonies of all the people of the empire and to suppress or kill dissenters. There is no material difference between the Roman emperors after Augustus Cæsar's time down to Theodosius (380 A.D.) and the Roman popes after the time of Theodosius. The only seeming difference is that the popes after 380 could not for a time make good their contention. In tracing the genealogy of the heads of the Roman Church we are not following the line of apostolic succession, but that of the Cæsarean lineage.

By no sort of torturing can Jewish priests be accused of usurping thrones or presidential chairs. If Christians are the spiritual descendants of Israel, there is not even a vestige of priestly claims among them. If the Jews as a race now preserve intact their ancient priestly prerogatives, there is no evidence that they religiously seek to control human governments.

THE RELIGION WHICH WAS BORN IN ITALY

There is only one prime issue in all the realm of religions; that is, as to the supremacy of morals over magic or the dominance of magic over morality. The Jewish religion conquered in this struggle and

Jesus Christ followed up the triumph with his match-
less system of morals and spirituality.

There was a time when the Italian religion faced
the same issue. The Romans of very ancient times
were hardy, industrious, healthy. Religion originally centered in the home. In any primitive cult morality has an important place. Among the Romans it
was the agricultural family which formed the basis
of national life.

The transition of early Roman life from the agricultural family to the city-state marked the new
epoch when ritualism became more elaborate, the
priests became a powerful caste, and the State became the basis of religion. That was the time when
the Roman Catholic Church was born. It was also
the time when the old Roman religion was hopelessly
vitiated. Says W. Warde Fowler:

Just when Roman history begins to be of absorbing interest, and fairly well substantiated, the Roman religion, as religion, has already begun to lose its vitality, its purity, its
efficacy. It has become overlaid with foreign rites and ideas,
and it has also become a religious monopoly of the State; of
which the essential characteristic, as Mommsen has well put
it, . . . was "the conscious retention of the principles of the
popular belief, which were recognized as irrational, for reasons
of outward convenience." It was not unlike the religion of
the Jews in the period immediately before the Captivity, and
it was never to profit by the chastening influence of such
lengthy suffering.[1]

Abraham left Ur of the Chaldees and founded the

----

[1]"The Religious Experience of the Roman People from the
Earliest Times to the Age of Augustus." The Gifford Lec-
tures for 1909–10. Delivered in Edinburgh University, by
W. Warde Fowler, M.A.

religion of Israel about 1900 B.C. Moses organized
the religion more fully some 700 years later (1200
B.C.).

Five or six hundred years after Moses's time the
great prophets, Amos, Isaiah, Jeremiah, and others
(750–600 B.C.), successfully attacked the ritualistic
practices and doctrines which had almost smothered
out the spiritual life of the Jews. It was precisely
at this period when prophecy was triumphing in the
religious struggle in Palestine that the reverse process
was going on in Italy. Mr. Fowler criticizes a certain writer who was misled into believing that the
Roman religion was "strongly moral," that "the
gods gave every man his duty and expected him to
perform it." Says he: "Here again no Roman of historical times, or indeed of any age, could have allowed this to be his creed. Had it really been so, not
only the history of Roman religion, but that of the
Roman State would have been very different from
what it actually was."

The magic and polytheism which were always in
Romanism were comparatively harmless as long as
they were under the control of the family priest. As
soon as the city-state arose and the priesthood became an institution separate from the household,
family piety became subordinate to the State,
policies took the place of personal purity, magic became an instrument of exploitation in the hands of
the priests, religion was the spiritual arm to be
wielded by the State. That was the beginning of the
Roman Catholic Church; Romanism has never
changed from then until now. In history we read of
the "secular arm." That is a misnomer; it is merely

the Catholic Church working in her proper sphere. Romanism has always been primarily a state affair; religion is simply an engine for the control of the masses by civil law, using, at the same time, spiritual threats and promises, not for spiritual or moral ends, but in order to substitute human for divine authority and to bring everything under the control of brute force.

Let us digress for a moment. Is it possible for a bad religion or for any other wicked institution to gain great power over large numbers of people and to continue wielding its authority through hundreds and thousands of years? The answer is that it has been done by various religions and governments. There are two principles of human nature which explain the marvelous duration of the despotic sway of a few men over multitudes of human beings; these are, a *desperately wicked ambition in the hearts of the few and an ingrained superstition in the hearts of the many*. As long as Czar, or Kaiser, or Caliph, or pope, or the old Roman Pontifex Maximus, from whom the pope's title of Pontiff is derived—or the emperor-god of China, Japan, or Peru could shut out the light of science and keep the moral code in the hands of the religious guides, they could cow the people with threats of punishment by angry gods. When the power of priests becomes so weakened that the people assert their right to think on scientific and moral and religious subjects, they select their own religious guides and their own political representatives. This has sometimes been largely a matter of evolution, but it has also been brought about by independent thinking and by courageous sacrifice. Blood and brains have been laid on the altar in the struggle for freedom from priests, from magic, and from kings.

The original Latins furnished the matrix in which the religion of the Roman Empire, later known as the Roman Catholic Church, was formed. The Sabines, an agricultural and grazing people, from the simplicity of their lives and their physical prowess "obtained a reputation like that of the Spartans for severity of discipline and sturdiness of character." These people no doubt had a very strong influence on the Romans at the very beginning of Roman life, before history gives any clear idea of it. It is probable that the original religion of the Romans was a blending of Latin and Sabine notions, with the Latin predominating.

While Romanism was trembling in the balance other influences pressed upon it from without and developed a religion of magic which has never changed and cannot change without self-destruction. If at its very incipiency original Romanism had taken the upward course, eliminating or subordinating ceremonialism, it could have joined hand in hand with Christianity to give to the world its ultimate religion as this was realized in Jesus Christ. But the original Latin religion was weak. When the influence of other cults was brought to bear on it, the polytheism and magic which were already in Romanism were driven deeper into the heart of the Italian cult, and this made a formal priesthood necessary.

The Etruscans were detrimental to Romanism. "Little can be said in favor of Etruscan morality. The men bore a reputation not merely for self-indulgent and luxurious habits, but for actual gluttony; and the women were said to be almost universally profligate. . . . Nor was this looseness of manners compensated for by softness of temper or gentleness of behavior toward others. The Etruscans were proverbially harsh in their treatment of their serf population, and often drove these wretched dependents into rebellion." Perhaps Romanism in Spain, in Mexico, and in South America during the past four hundred years has been reincarnating the cruelties of her Etruscan ancestors.

Some Interesting Features of the Ancient Religion of Italy

The Catholic religion has been charged with being one-third Christian, one-third Jewish, and one-third heathen. That is erroneous. The Christian elements which appear to be in Romanism cannot be considered as having any part at all, because they cannot consort with her vital pagan elements. For instance, it cannot be right and wrong at the same time to gamble and steal. It is impossible that there should be only one God and at the same time a multiplicity of saints and popes and a great goddess— the Virgin Mary—with the divine powers which these have in Romanism. That would be as impossible as that two and two are four, and at the same time five. To recognize the code of morals taught by Jesus makes it impossible to admit the authority of Romish casuistry. He who attempts to follow the moral standards of good men and of thieves at the same time only adopts the iniquitous doctrines of the thieves.

Once it is shown, as we have done, that Romanism

has in her all the seven vital elements of pure heathenism, it can never be proven that she has any of the important principles of Christianity.

It is not necessary to search among the Jews for anything of importance in Romanism. Not only all the inveterate qualities of Catholicism are to be found in the old religion of Italy, but many incidental marks of identity are to be traced to that peninsula.

The worship of family gods "was almost the only part of Roman religion that was not flooded and obscured by the inrush of Oriental cults." Romanism in her little saints reproduces this old idea of family gods.

The foundation of Romanism, both pagan and papal, is the State. (1) The fetial was a semi-political priestly board. Its duties were to supervise the rites peculiar to the declaration of war and the swearing of treaties. (2) The aggressive world policy of the Catholic Church is purely the original world policy of Rome. The methods and purposes are the same. (3) That the foreigners should support the Romans in their idleness is precisely the policy now of the Italian bishops toward the Catholics of the Americas. (4) The old Roman notion of the supremacy of law is now replaced by the Romish doctrine of the supremacy of dogma. This is shown in the Creed of Pius IV., in which the ordinary Church member is required to state that he accepts a complicated system of dogma which he never can understand even in the most superficial manner. The average Catholic will never know even the titles of the doctrines which he says he believes. And such a pretended belief is what Romish theologians call

5

"faith." (5) The complete absorption of the individual in the State is an old Roman trait; the complete surrender of private judgment to the hierarchy is the modern form of the same thing. (6) The heads of Church and State were finally merged into one, when the title of Pontifex Maximus (or chief of the pontifices) was conferred on the emperor. That is the doctrine of the Romish Church now. The head of the State, as an official who is inferior to the head of the Church, has his place, but it is marked out to him by his superior. (7) As a result of this position, the Romans accused the Christians of atheism and treason because they ignored the gods and refused to perform emperor worship. This was the cause of most of the early anti-Christian persecutions. In the same manner the Romanists have systematically charged dissenters with irreligion and treason because they denied the small gods (or saints) and refused to perform emperor worship—that is, submission to the pope. (8) Pagan Rome tolerated other religions because they were subservient to the State religion. Romanism claims to be the "mother and mistress of all churches," and this under the *peculiar* protection of the civil government. (9) The organization of the Catholic Church is fashioned on the old Roman State, with the pope at the head and exercising absolute power, regardless of its iniquitous character, and transmitting from above downward full authority through his subordinates. The Roman emperor brooked no rival and his authority was not conditioned on its justice. Two things were required in all the Roman world—to wit, unquestioned obedience, regardless of justice, and the payment of taxes, however extortionate they might be. In the same way modern Romanism demands unquestioned obedience to both good and bad popes, and payment for ecclesiastical gewgaws.

The same vestments which were used in pagan Rome are now used by Romish priests.

That ministering vestments, properly so-called, and with them ecclesiastical insignia, were unknown among Christians of the apostolic age may be considered as unquestionably certain; and in like manner, in the three succeeding centuries only the faintest traces, if indeed any authentic traces whatever, of such vestments can be said either to exist, or to have left indications of ever having existed. . . . Even at the commencement of the ninth century, when the true historical era of ecclesiastical costume may be defined to have commenced with it, the two most remarkable circumstances in connection with ecclesiastical costume were, on the one hand, its approximately unchanged character, and, on the other hand, its close general resemblance, amounting almost to identity, to the old civil costume, which in the state dresses of the Roman official dignitaries survived the sweeping changes of barbarian revolution.[2]

The same article points out that it is remarkable that "the Christian [meaning the Romish] hierarchy should have derived the insignia of their rank in the Church, through the high position of civil power in the State exercised by the early bishops of Rome, from the official decorations of the Roman magistracy as well of the republic as of the empire."

The Latin language—that of the Romans—is used to-day by papal Rome in the face of the prohibition by Paul of the use of an "unknown tongue" in worship and in precisely the way which led its use to be prohibited by the Apostle.

---

[2]Encyclopedia Britannica, Ninth Edition, Vol. VI., page 461.

It is very significant that the same city which was the head of pagan Rome should be regarded with a sort of superstitious reverence as the head of Romanism now.

Purple and red were colors specially used by the pagan priesthood among the Italians before Christ, so their prevalence to-day among the Catholic priesthood is another indication of the solidarity of the system, ancient and modern.

A strong tendency to atheism among the intellectuals was germinally in Italian Romanism; it bore fruit as the State religion developed. Celsus (178?), the great protagonist in the Romish fight on Christianity, was a prototype of many popes, bishops, and especially mercenary Romish laymen of later times, of the Middle Ages, and of the modern period.

His main concern is the Roman State, . . . doubly threatened by passive disaffection of Christianity within its borders. . . . It was immaterial what private opinions he might hold, for his great purpose was the abandonment of particularism and the fusion of all parties for the general good. Private judgment run mad was the mark of all Christians, orthodox and heretical—"men walling themselves off and isolating themselves from mankind"—and his thesis was that the whole spirit of the movement was wrong. A good citizen's part was loyal acceptance of the common belief, deviation from which was not shown to impair the solidarity of the civilized world.[3]

How exact is that a description of Charles V., his son Philip II., Francis I., Henry VIII., and other monsters who were logical products of Romanism!

Infatuation for old forms of religion is extraordina-

[3]"The Conflict of Religions in the Early Roman Empire," by P. R. Glover, page 240.

ry among Romans, ancient and modern. It is duly
proclaimed in the Syllabus (1864 A.D.) in the 80th
Proposition: "The Roman Pontiff cannot and ought
not to reconcile himself to, and agree with, progress,
liberalism, and civilization as lately introduced."
Popes have systematically fought and hated democratic governments ever since their beginnings.
Says Mr. Fowler, as to the ancient Romans:

They clung with extraordinary tenacity, all through their
history, to old forms. . . . It would be easy to illustrate this
curious feature of the Roman mind from the history of its religion; it never disappeared; and to this day the Catholic
Church in Italy retains in a thinly disguised form many of the
religious practices of the early Roman people.[4]

Infant baptism as a means of purification is an
Italian practice. "Every Roman child needed purification or disinfection: boys on the ninth, girls on the
eighth, day after birth. This day was called the *dies
lustricus*, the day of a purificatory rite." Romanists
practice infant baptism in order to save the child
from *limbus infantum*.

Holy wells were common, "which were honored
with models of the limbs their waters healed, and
other curious gifts thrown into them." That custom
has been continued by Romanists down to the present time. However, the priests have managed to
turn all the gifts to themselves; they are too thrifty
to have gifts wasted on holy wells.

Tithes were not first invented by the Jews or the
Catholics; they were exacted in Italy at a very early
date.

Exorcism for the protection of beasts on the farm

---

[4]"Religious Experience of the Roman People," page 25.

is a present-day Catholic practice which dates back to Italy many centuries before Christ.

The sign of the cross for protection against devils is purely Romish, duly authorized in their books of devotion. Says Mr. Fowler: "Professor von Duhn told me that once when approaching an Italian village in search of inscriptions he was taken for the devil, being unluckily mounted on a black horse and dressed in black, and was met by a priest with a crucifix, who was at last persuaded to 'disinfect' him with holy water as a condition of his being admitted to the village."[5]

The Catholic law that a priest must not shed blood is an Italian trait. Says Fowler: "The shedding of blood, except when a victim was sacrificed under the rules of sacred law, was carefully avoided; thus the horror of blood had a social and ethical result of value, instead of remaining a mere *religio* (taboo)."

Holy places—some (*sacra*) consecrated by the State, and therefore of prime importance; others (*religiosa*), such as shrines, belonging to families and gentes, and temple-sites in the provinces of a later age—were common in Italy and are now common in genuine Catholic countries.

"All burial grounds were not *loca sacra,* but *loca religiosa,* technically because they were not the property of the State or consecrated by it; in reality, I venture to say because the place where a corpse was deposited was of necessity taboo." Romanism continues the same ancient heathen custom of having holy burying grounds; more than that, the clergy make capital out of it by persuading their devotees

---

[5] "Religious Experience of the Roman People," page 31.

that such a sacred resting place for the body has
something to do with the felicity of the soul.

The days of the Parentalia in February and the
Lemuria in May were concerned with the cult and
the memory of the dead. Romanism has settled on
November 1 as All Saints' Day and November 2
as All Souls' Day.[6]

The Romish idea of the Communion of Saints is
also about the same as the original Italian notion of
communion with the dead.

The Vestal Virgins have been superseded by Romish nuns. Their power to set criminals free has been
reproduced, during and since the Middle Ages, in the
power of the Virgin Mary to free criminals.

The bulla is a small object inclosed in a capsule and
suspended around a child's neck to protect him
against evil spirits. Says Fowler: "A kind of
harmless magic, to which the Romans, like all
Italians, ancient and modern, were peculiarly ad-
dicted, is the use of amulets. Here there is no spell,
or obvious and expressed exercise of will power on
the part of the individual, but the potent influence,
mana, or whatever we choose to call it, resides in a
material object which brings good luck, like the cast
horseshoe of our own times, or protects against
hostile will power, and especially against the evil
eye. This curious and widespread superstition was

---

[6]Something equivalent to All Souls' Day is observed in
China, where benevolent people during the Tsing Ming festival—the worship at the graves about our Easter time—offer
food also to the spirits of beggars, persons lost at sea, to all
spirits, in fact, whose bodies could not receive burial or who
have left no descendants to perform the filial offices at their
or before their ancestral tablets.

probably the *raison d'etre* of most of the amulets worn or carried by Romans. A modern Italian, even if he be a complete skeptic and materialist, will probably be found to have some amulet about him against the evil eye, 'just to be on the safe side.'"[7]

As is well known, amulets and various other kinds of charms are worn by children and older people also in heathen lands, so Rome does not have a monopoly on such superstitions.

Devoutness in religion and immorality in conduct came to be a very natural thing in pagan Rome. Mr. Fowler says: "That the formalized religion of later times had become almost divorced from morality there is indeed no doubt." That is notoriously true of genuine Romanism to-day, but it is not all of the truth. If Romanists were merely permitted to practice iniquities, the case would not be so bad; but they are advised or even required, in some cases, to practice sin and crime in order to be religious.

There is one peculiar phase of Pagan Rome which relieves in some measure the harshness of Catholicism. "It may be said," remarks Mr. Fowler, "without going beyond the truth, that the religion of the family remained the same in all essentials throughout Roman history, and the great priesthoods of the State never interfered with it in any such degree as to affect its vitality." If it were true that the Roman Catholic priesthood had not in any way affected the integrity of the family, we might possibly have hope that family piety and purity could reassert itself as against the priesthood of the city-state. But it is only in a measure that the family has been able to

---

[7] "Religious Experience of the Roman People," pages 60, 61.

guard itself against the encroachments of the Catholic clergy. It is to the credit of many men in Catholic countries that they do not allow their wives and daughters to go to the confessional.

Names, titles, words have been reproduced in modern Romanism.

A *curia* was a subdivision of an old Latin tribe; also a place of assembly for the *curia*. The same word is now used to designate a papal court.

The very words "pontifex maximus" were used by ancient Romans to designate the chief of a group of special priests; the word "pontiff" now means the chief papal priest.

It is noteworthy that the priesthood was not hereditary in Italy, just as it is not now hereditary in Romanism.

Old Romans forbade marriage during the month of May; modern Romanism prohibits it during Lent or Advent.

The striking resemblances between old Italian religious customs and later Roman Catholic features are only presumptive proofs of the identity between Papal Paganism and Roman Paganism. The demonstration rests on the continuity of the original seven congenital qualities which have never been absent at any time from the religion which we now know as the Roman Catholic and which was known in Italy twenty-five hundred years ago as the religion of the Romans.

CHAPTER III

THE PAGAN ENLARGEMENT OF ROMANISM

THE main reason why Romanism is so hard to understand is that it is a composite; elements mutually contradictory are so jumbled up in a conglomerate mass as to lead one astray until he finds the key to it all. No other religion has undertaken seriously to blend Christian with heathen elements. For instance, the Apostles' Creed is bound up with the Creed of Pius IV., as if the two could both be true. But this very incongruity is a Romish trait. Beginning and ending with magic as basic, Rome yet undertakes to graft on Christianity, which has righteousness for its goal; a task as hopeless as it would be to "gather grapes of thorns or figs of thistles." This strange procedure is also seen in her absorption of other religions:

The primitive religious (or magico-religious) instinct, which was the germ of the religion of the historical Romans, was gradually atrophied by over-elaboration of ritual, but showed itself again in strange forms from the period of the Punic Wars onward.[1]

Again:

Roman law expanded *organically* and intensively, absorbing into its own body the experience and practice of other peoples, while Roman religion expanded *mechanically* and extensively, by taking on the deities and worship of others without any organic change of its own being. . . . Roman religion, though

---

[1] "Religious Experience of the Roman People," page vii.

(74)

it eventually admitted the ideas and cults of Greeks and others, did so without taking them by a digestive process into its own system.

If the ancient Roman religion had really absorbed into itself the principles brought to it from Greek and Oriental faiths, the probabilities are that she could have surrendered to Christianity. The paganism which came into rivalry with Christianity was much more advanced than the Italian religion. Says M. Cumont:

> The mass of religions at Rome finally became so impregnated by neo-Platonism and Orientalism that paganism may be called a single religion with a fairly distinct theology, whose doctrines were somewhat as follows: adoration of the elements, especially the cosmic bodies; the reign of one God, eternal and omnipotent, with messenger attendants; spiritual interpretation of the gross rites yet surviving from primitive times; assurance of eternal felicity to the faithful; belief that the soul was on earth to be proved before its final return to the universal spirit, of which it was a spark; the existence of an abysmal abode for the evil, against whom the faithful must keep up an unceasing struggle; the destruction of the universe, the death of the wicked, and the eternal happiness of the good in a reconstructed world.[2]

The pagan theology above delineated was an improvement on Italian paganism and might have been made a bridge over which the religion of the empire could deliver itself over to the faith which originated in Palestine, which was purified and saved from the supremacy of magic by the great prophets, and which was perfected by the Man of Galilee. But the fatal flaw of priestly flummery, usurping the function of conscience and transferring it to the State, made this impossible.

---

[2]"Oriental Religions in Roman Paganism," pages 8, 9.

Since religion deals with an unseen world, a future life, and an invisible God, we must either surrender to the claims of wonder-workers as such or we must demand that all theology walk the earth. Whatever else may be claimed for Christianity, we must insist on its unique place as a religion of righteousness. The resurrection of the dead, the miracles of Christ, the inspiration of Scripture all go for nought if they do not contribute to the ethical life.

All this is the exact reverse of the philosophy of Romanism, both ancient and modern. The most important doctrine of Romanism is the magical power of the priesthood in the realm of religion. The whole of Italian paganism in its practical aspects may be summed up in three items: (1) The ability of the pope to define moral doctrines and to control human conduct without personal righteousness; (2) the authority of the priest to perform the sacraments validly to the saving of souls, without personal righteousness; and (3) the preparation of the penitent for the reception of absolution without perfect repentance. All this is diametrically opposed to the doctrine of Jesus Christ. (1) Jesus himself asks that we accept him because he lived a righteous life as a basis for all his claims. (2) The ministry authorized by Christ must be judged by its fruits—righteousness and not wonder-working power is basic. (3) Repentance is absolutely required as a condition of forgiveness.

George Adam Smith has pointed out that ceremonialism is the foundation of all the evils of heathenism. Says he:

When one is asked, What is the distinguishing characteristic of heathenism? one is always ready to say, Idolatry, which is not true. The distinguishing characteristic of heathenism is the stress which it lays upon ceremonial. To the pagan religions, both of the ancient and of the modern worlds, rites were the indispensable elements in religion. The gifts of the gods, the abundance of fruits, the security of the State, depended upon the full and accurate performance of ritual. In Greek literature we have innumerable illustrations of this: the Iliad itself starts from a god's anger, roused by an insult to his priest, whose prayers for vengeance he hears because sacrifices have been assiduously offered to him. And so too with the systems of paganism from which the faith of Israel, though at first it had so much in common with them, broke away to its supreme religious distinction. The Semites laid the stress of their obedience to the gods upon traditional ceremonies; and no sin was held so heinous by them as the neglect or infringement of a religious rite. By the side of it offenses against one's fellow-men or one's own character were deemed mere misdemeanors. In the day of Amos this pagan superstition thoroughly penetrated the religion of Jehovah, and so absorbed the attention of men that without the indignant and complete repudiation of it prophecy could not have started on her task of identifying morality with religion. . . . Idolatries die everywhere; but everywhere a superstitious ritualism survives. It continues with philosophies that have ceased to believe in the gods who enforced it. . . . Ritual is a thing which appeals both to the baser and to the nobler instincts of man. To the baser it offers itself as a mechanical atonement for sin, and a substitute for all moral and intellectual effort in connection with faith; to the nobler it insists on a man's need in religion of order and routine, of sacrament and picture.[3]

Ritual turns morality upside down. Socrates was forced to drink the hemlock because he put knowledge and morals above ceremonies and idolatry, and yet he was accused of corrupting the youth. But while Socrates died his philosophy lived. Why did

---

[3] "The Book of the Twelve Prophets," comment on Amos iv., etc.

not Greek thought merge with Christianity and become purified by it? Because the Italian religion, after it had absorbed Greek philosophy, reached its culmination in emperor worship and then by the power of the State forced its ritual on the people to the extermination of conscience. Emperor worship was the climax of polytheism, ceremonialism, and priestcraft; it was the triumph of the Italian religion which began its world career with the rise of the city-state. The supremacy and infallibility of the Romish pope is precisely the same thing as emperor worship; it is the substitution for Christianity of the notion that the State has the right to prescribe religious beliefs and practices to the individual and to force unity throughout the world.

All religions must face the issue between magic and morals. Judaism was saved by the preaching of the prophets between the eighth and the sixth centuries B.C. and by her suffering in Babylon. Greece was brought to the borderland of salvation by her philosophers about the same time or a little later. Rome passed her crisis during the seventh and sixth centuries before the Christian era; then it was that the die was cast; she could not be saved because she was intoxicated with her success as a world power. Had Augustine's "City of God" been built on righteousness instead of priestly thaumaturgy and imperial savagery, it would not have stood through the centuries merely as a castle in the air.

Christianity has suffered irreparable loss because her friends have encouraged the idea that she has been represented by the Roman Catholic Church. The heathen elements in Romanism are not incidental; they did not begin with Christ. Romanism is not paganized Christianity; it is pure paganism. The distinctive features which mark Romanism to-day as a cult are entirely different from the Chrisrianity of the first centuries and equally different from the Christianity of the twentieth century. To charge the Christian religion with the Crusades or with the persecution of heretics, especially with the murder of the Albigenses and the Huguenots, is to contradict the plain principles of logic.

1. *The nature of the Roman Catholic gods is heathen.*

(1) The chief god of Romanism is the contribution of Zoroastrianism, of the Egyptians, the Greeks, and the Romans.

Zoroastrianism has given to Rome an imperfect, yet withal a very decent, great god, Ahura Mazda. He has degenerated considerably since attaching himself to the Catholic Church, but he retains three characteristics: (a) As with Ahura Mazda, the supreme god of Romanism is worshiped without images; (b) both of these deities permit pantheons of smaller gods; (c) in each cult, the lesser deities are worshiped through the medium of idols. The hurt which Ahura Mazda sustained after becoming the Romish chief deity consists in the plenary powers he has conferred on the priesthood and the persistent Italian magic which they always wield and which results in a thorough system of iniquitous casuistry.

The Egyptian religions developed a chief god, Re, who was similar to Ahura Mazda. Egypt scarcely reached a pure monotheism; the highest god had a precarious rank. He had to join himself to inferior deities. "In the end almost every Egyptian god had a public cult hyphenated with Re." So the Catholic almighty is joined with Mary, the pope, and certain saints in a very compromising way. The Egyptian great gods were infinitely above most of the little gods. This is the case with Romanism; the great god is far higher than the saints. The special contribution of Egypt was a god who must operate almost entirely through a priesthood on whom was conferred tremendous authority.

The Greek Absolute was, for many centuries, the supreme deity of Romanism. This was slightly modified by Thomas Aquinas, but Rome still has a cold, cruel great god who would turn his subordinates loose on the world as in the days of the Inquisition, were he not afraid of public opinion.

Jupiter, the greatest Roman god, was primarily a deity of power, and secondarily of goodness. The old rascal was a scapegrace when his consort, Juno, relaxed her discipline. If a god may be known by his fruits, the principal deity of the Romish Church may very properly be regarded as a modernized Jupiter. He cannot be called good as long as the Catholic Church represents him through its authorized teaching and discipline.

(2) Lesser gods are common to all non-Christian religions except Mohammedanism. These small gods have no higher rank among heathen than the saints have among Romanists. In both cases they are far nearer to human beings than they are to the chief deity.

D'Alviella points out that "if the idea of an *only god* can be reconciled with the real existence of terrestrial beings, there is no reason why it should not harmonize equally well with the belief in *intermediate beings, superior to human nature, but taking part in the affairs of the world.*"

Some of these little deities are barely superior to human beings. "The worship which a Confucianist performs before the tablet of an ancestor or a sage signifies little more than our lifting of the hat at the tomb of a hero or saint."[4]

The fact that the saints derive all their power from the great god is also heathen in its origin. In China at the head of their system "stands Shang-ti, the celestial emperor who watches over the general interests of the world. . . . Confucius declares that the functionaries of the State are the servants of heaven, just as the Liki says (Book of Rites) that *the spirits are the functionaries of Shang-ti.*"[5]

Mary and the saints have been *exalted* to their high places by a natural process. Ancestor worship in Siberia, China, and elsewhere follows the same line of development. Æsculapius among the Greeks grew from a skillful physician to be the "guide and governor of the Universe, preserver of the World, and guardian of the Immortal Gods."[6]

The Chinese have long believed that by worshiping their ancestors they exalt them and thus greatly improve their condition in Hades.

The pope, though a lesser god, is an obstreperous deity who on occasion manages to ignore the highest god. This he does when absolving his devotees from

---

[4]"The Religions of the World," Barton, page 240; see also page 307.

[5]"Growth of the Conception of God," D'Alviella, page 152.

[6]*Ibid.*, page 131.

6

oaths, also when commanding his subjects to rob and murder in the name of religion. These prerogatives are inherited from Egypt. On the walls of the tomb of an Egyptian king, 2655–2625 B.C., are to be found these words: "King Unis is the one who eats men and lives on gods. . . . He hath swallowed the knowledge of every god."[7]

The Catholic pontiff, by his infallibility, has virtually "swallowed the knowledge" of his highest god.

The peculiar character of the papal divinity is Egyptian in its origin. "The king was not a plain mortal like his subjects, but was himself *Horus* in human form, an incarnation of the deity, and he bore a name expressive of the fact. He ruled, therefore, by divine right and was addressed with titles of divinity, but *there is no indication that religious worship was paid to the living ruler.*"[8]

It is a remarkable fact that Romanism has three classes of gods, corresponding roughly to the three classes in ancient Rome, viz.: "Those of the poet, those of the philosopher, and those of the statesman."[9]

The gods of the poets were similar to the miracle-working saints; those of the philosopher are reproduced in the authoritative teachers of the early Church, the fathers and medieval theologians; those of the statesman are now represented by the pope, the priest, and the Virgin Mary, who combine to

[7]"The Religions of the World," Barton, pages 338, 339.
[8]"History of Religions," Moore, Vol. I., page 150.
[9]*Ibid.*, page 561.

control civil government and keep the masses in ignorance.

Notice the mode of transition: "Old gods were in many places christened as Christian saints, and their cults were maintained under a Christian name."[10]

"By the fourth century it was believed that the blessed martyrs, through communion with our Lord, shared in his attributes of omnipresence and omniscience. Prayer in behalf of the saints changed to prayers to them for help. This transition was particularly easy for those who were won from paganism because they were already accustomed to similar practices."[11]

Functional deities are universal in pagan faiths. Practical Romanism illustrates this fact. A standard Romish handbook mentions a few special functions of certain saints. Joseph is "Custodian and Father of virgins;" the archangel Saint Rafael is the "medicine of God, health of the sick, light of the blind, guide of travelers, protector of charity, fasting, and prayer;" St. Anthony of Padua is the god of "lost articles." St. Roque is god of "all contagious diseases" and St. Emigdios is the "special advocate against earthquakes."[12]

The following gods are also common: Isidore, of farmers; Lucretia, of sore eyes; St. George, of snake-bites and dog-bites. Erasmus calls attention to Rochus, who drove plagues from the body; Apollonia, the god of toothache; and Job, the savior from itch. He sees little difference between those Catholic de-

---

[10]"History of Religions," Moore, Vol. I., page 324.

[11]"The Rise of the Medieval Church," Flick, page 378.

[12]"The Manual of Devotion to Our Lady of Perpetual Help."

votions and original paganism—*e. g.*, a vow to Hercules in order to get rich, or a cock to Æsculapius to recover from an illness, or the slaying of a bull to Neptune for a favorable voyage.[13]

So also in China there are numerous gods representing every profession and avocation; such as, the god of sailors, the god of gamblers, the god of thieves, etc.

Departmental deities are both Romish and heathen—*e. g.*, St. Patrick of Ireland, Mary is a war goddess in many countries.

Some heathen deities are objects of terror during their lifetime. Rome has gods of this sort in those Inquisitors who have been exalted into saints.

(3) Goddesses are also numerous among non-Christian cults. They represent motherhood, virginity, chastity, sympathy, and mercy. They lead in war, protect their devotees, and preside over purgatory, or hell, or the nether world. They are vain, emotional, active, and meddlesome. They provoke war, free the guilty from punishment, and excite the most violent passions, especially of men. The worship of Mary has a multiform origin.

The *Zoroastrians* worshiped *Anahita* as a mother-goddess.

The *Ægeans* adored *Rhea* as *Anahita* was venerated. According to Hesiod she was *the mother of Zeus*.

Among the *Babylonians*, *Ishtar* went to the nether world to recover her lost lover, *Tammuz*. That is somewhat similar to Mary, who goes down to purgatory every Saturday to bring out all her devotees.

Artemis, often called the "Huntress," was a Greek

---

[13]"History of the Reformation," Lindsey, Vol. I., page 180.

goddess of wild nature. Like Mary, she gave easy childbirth, also a safe and prosperous voyage to mariners. From the time of Homer, she was chaste. In that she was a type of Mary. *Athena was one of the greatest of Greek gods;* "in Homer she is second only to Zeus." She was *warlike. Demeter, "Mother Earth,"* was a *Greek goddess who was connected with the nether world.*

The goddesses of *Nineveh, Assyria, Syria,* and *Asia Minor* were warlike. So Mary is the chastening rod of heretics; a fierce partisan in battle. Her flag among Catholic troops creates a frenzied hatred of the enemy; she has the same faculty of inflaming the minds of her devotees that the imaginary Dulcinea of Don Quixote had to topple the rickety reason of that famous Spanish ninny. This is a reproduction of the insane cry, "Great is Diana of the Ephesians," and is no less heathen in its results.

At the head of the Shinto pantheon is the sun goddess, much as Mary heads the Catholic pantheon.

In *Buddhism, Kwannon* is the goddess of mercy, like Mary in Romanism.

Mary is similar to the *Vedic goddesses* in that she and they alike are dependent on the supreme deity.

The goddesses of Civaism in India are active powers of the *supreme God.* "The god himself abides, as philosophers say he should, in bliss untroubled by the administration of a universe; while his 'energies' in female personification . . . are the efficient cause of all that comes to pass in the world." Romish theologians grant Mary a sort of universal sway among human activities and natural phenomena. In genuine Catholic countries Mary is by far the most active member of the coterie of divinities. This coterie consists of the Father, the Son, the Holy Ghost the Pope, and Mary.

Sodalities in honor of Mary were first instituted when Cybele, the Phrygian mother of the gods, was admitted to a place in the Roman State religion in 204 B.C. "At the great festival in the spring Roman gentlemen's clubs (sodalities) dined together in commemoration of the importation of the goddess." These sodalities are, and have always been, hotbeds of fanaticism.

The distinction between the subordination of Mary and the inferiority of heathen goddesses is insignificant. Practically all goddesses, and most gods as well, have their beginnings; they have their limitations; they depend upon a god who is higher than they, or on a vague, eternal, original force, or god, conceived of as back of all phenomena and all gods. Jupiter had a beginning. "Saturn (Chronos) was his father and Rhea (Ops) was his mother. Saturn and Rhea were of the race of Titans, who were the children of Earth and Heaven, while Chaos is back of all the gods." This places Juno *fifth* from the original source of power and divinity. Mary is only *second* or *third;* sometimes between Jehovah and Jesus and sometimes scarcely lower than Christ. The distinction between the attitude of those pagan goddesses to their superiors and that of Mary to her master is that in the latter case the goddess is more cultured and deferential than was Juno or any other goddess of those barbarous times. It is analogous to the old-fashioned woman and the modern woman; both manage their husbands, the former without his know-

ing it, while the latter announces the fact. Mary
follows the old method. The introduction to the
book of Canticles, also the introduction to the chap-
ters of the book, in the Douay Bible show that the
Romish Church regards |Mary as both the mother
and the spouse of Jesus Christ. Mary is really
greater than Juno, the consort of Jupiter, or Hera,
the sister and wife of Zeus; her dominion is vaster
and her authority is freer from interference by her
spouse than are theirs.   She is called "Queen of the
world," "Queen of heaven," "Queen of all saints,"
"Queen of hell and of all evil spirits," "Mother of
God and men."

The introduction of foreign goddesses into Rome
about two hundred years before Christ was because
of the decay of faith and because of the hope that the
bringing in of emotional cults would restore it. The
Magna Mater of Phrygia and also Isis and other
Oriental goddesses were brought to Rome for that
purpose. The virulence of Mariolatry during and
since the counter Reformation is due to the same decay of faith.

Isis is the immediate progenitor of the Virgin
Mary. Although not the greatest deity of Egypt,
yet, by the method of *henotheism*, just as in the case
of Mary, she makes herself the greatest, for the time
being, while she is being implored. In the mysteries
of Isis she appears in all the radiance of her divinity
and declares:

I who am parent of nature, the supreme among divinities,
the queen of departed spirits, the first of the celestials, and the
uniform manifestation of the gods and goddesses; who govern
by my nod the luminous heights of heaven, the salubrious

streams, and the anguished silent realms of the world below; whose one sole divinity the whole orb of the earth venerates under a manifold form, with different rites, and under a variety of appellations.[14]

Modern Catholics hold that Protestants may be saved without consciously worshiping Mary. But Catholic standards make it impossible for any one to be saved without the *intervention* of Mary. It follows that all must worship Mary either knowingly or ignorantly. This reproduces that characteristic of Isis which allows the whole orb to venerate her "under a manifold form, with different rites, and a variety of appellations."

As rivals of Christianity from the second to the fourth centuries, no cult, except that of Mithras, equaled those of Magna Mater and Isis. Likewise the worshipers of Mary are now the bitterest opponents of Christianity in the world. The Virgin is the goddess of modern popes, the patron of the Jesuits, and the favorite of the diabolical casuist, Liguori. She therefore controls the political head, the active missionary force, and the whole ethical system of Romanism.

After the cult of Isis had been introduced into Rome and the public mind had become saturated with the idea of an indispensable goddess it was only a step to the invention of a so-called Christian goddess.

A king of heaven had been revealed, but where was the queen? Her throne stood empty. . . . Men did not think of calling God our Father and Mother as Theodore Parker used to do. The heretical sects again and again introduced some female saint or heavenly being, a Helena or such-like

---

[14] "History of Religions," Moore, Vol. I., page 690.

imaginary creature, to the notice of the Christian public; but the void was not filled up, and the demand for a goddess was increasingly felt, as ignorant converts pressed into the Church under the Christian emperors. At length, in some of the controversies of the fourth century, attention was almost accidentally drawn to the position of the Virgin Mother. The subtle disputes about the nature of the God-man drew men's thoughts to Mary, at once, just as in the electrotype process, the floating paganism, which hung diluted in the spirit of the times, precipitated itself around her figure as a center, and overlaid the simple Mary of Nazareth, as she appears in the Gospel, with a gorgeous and elaborate chasing of variegated superstition. By a curious felicity every traditional feeling, every passionate longing of the old faith, found what it needed in some aspect of the Virgin Mary. As Virgin, she gratified the admiration for maidenly purity expressed in the worship of Minerva and the chaste Diana, the latter resigning to her the crescent moon, which a happy misapplication of the Apocalypse placed beneath her feet. As mother (of God) she realized the aspirations of the devotees of Cybele, mother of the gods, and Demeter, the sorrowing parent, whose grief for Proserpine was perpetuated in her dolors at the cross. Like Vesta she was priestess to perpetual virginity. A queen of heaven like Juno, she is like Venus Aphrodite, connected with the sea by a false etymology of her name. She also has somehow appropriated a star like the old Grecian deity, and is much worshiped by mariners as the star of the sea.

Women bewail her griefs as they did those of Venus Astarte for Adonis or Tammuz. As Spouse, by some wresting of the Canticles, she is no less renowned, and is as much worshiped in the Levant as ever Isis was; and here, too, the dolors find a place for the sorrows of Isis for her murdered husband which was every year commemorated by a solemn fast. Nor are howlings at night wanting to complete her resemblance to Hecate, as Ford has justly remarked in speaking of Spanish customs.

This strange metamorphosis of the modest, retiring woman, Mary, into a gaudy, bustling, interfering, spiritual potentate,

delighting in fine clothes and coarse flattery, was first encouraged by a council at Ephesus, which has been for ages the
seat of the worship of the Virgin goddess, and it was finally
sanctioned by another council held in Bythinia, the favorite
haunt of the Idean mother of the gods and her followers, the
Corybantes.[15]

(4) Image worship came directly from the heathen;
it was neither invented nor modified by Romanism,
but simply absorbed.

So far as we know, image worship is everywhere a
comparatively modern practice. China, Rome, and
Japan in their early religious careers were evidently
without man-made idols. Taoism borrowed its
images from Buddhism. Horus, in Egypt, had a seat
which he was supposed to occupy, but with no idol
sitting in it. Images in Zoroastrianism came as a
later development.

The evils of such gross worship were appreciated
long ago, not only by Jews and Christians, but by
others. Among the Greeks the Stoics "declared the
whole public cultus, with its images and sacrifices,
not only senseless but harmful." In India idolatry
was assailed in the fifteenth century among Hindus
and Mohammedans. The evil was not entirely
cured; the whole problem waits on Christianity for
its solution.

Differentiation between the god and the object in
which it dwelt was "made to order" for Romanism
by earlier cults. Says D'Alviella:

From the very first, worship must have been addressed, not
to the material object conceived as such, but to the personality

---

[15]See an article by N. B. Batt, in the *Contemporary Review*,
Vol. 13, pages 346–361, for 1870.

supposed to be embodied in it. . . . In Polynesia they make figures of carved wood into which the priests inject the souls of the dead or those of the gods according to taste. . . . Many peoples believe that the souls of the deceased pass by preference into the statues or portraits made in their own likeness. . . . Among the Papuans, when anyone dies, the survivors go to the neighboring forest and cut a statuette or *Korwar* out of a bit of wood, and then they invite the spirit to come and live in it.[16]

Various other methods of getting the spirit into the object are given by D'Alviella. In old Calabar it is done by exposing the fetishes to the open air; other negro tribes use the hocus-pocus; among the Finns, the doll must be carried nine times around the Church, with the cry, "Synna para" (Para, be born). In Romanism the image must represent Jesus, Mary. or a regularly canonized saint; it must be of the proper material and figure; it must be duly blessed by a member of the hierarchy who has been consecrated by one who is in the apostolical succession. All the requisites—proper vestments, postures, genuflections, words, etc.—must be observed. Evidence from various Catholic sources is abundant that official Romanism recognizes the presence of the saint in the image after it has been thrilled by Catholic theurgy or divine wonder-working power.

Since the highest authorities in the Romish Church deliberately make of the image either a transient or permanent dwelling place for the god or saint, it is not strange that to the common herd "a saint or madonna that rolls its eyes, drops tears, sheds blood, speaks, inflicts diseases or wards them off, and sends

[16]See "Growth of the Conception of God," pages 97, 99, 112, 115, 116.

rain or fine weather to the fields, is as much an idol—
that is to say, a fetish in human form—as the veriest
fetish or fetishes amongst the negroes, whether in
human form or not."[17]

George Trumbull Ladd holds precisely the same
view as that held by D'Alviella.[18]

He quotes in the same strain Max Müller, and also
Howard. The latter states:

Apparently the lowest fetishism does not identify its god
with the thing-like representation. . . . An unwarranted dis-
respect to the intelligence of the most degraded savages is
done when they are virtually accused of incapacity for making
those distinctions which are necessary for even the lowest form
of religion.

George Foot Moore teaches the same thing.
Speaking of Hinduism, he says:

As in other countries, these objects become holy after a
priest, with appropriate rites, has invited the god to lodge in
them.[19]

A sort of patronizing air, coupled with contempt
for the idol, was also inherited by Romanists from
their heathen and savage predecessors. Says Ladd:

For generations in the Roman Catholic communities of
southern Europe the common people have been ready to treat
the images of their saints as the savages of Australia and Polynesia treat their fetishes, when they fail to respond to their
prayers for help.[20]

D'Alviella has noted similar phenomena. "In
China," says he, "when an idol is tardy in rendering

---

[17]See "Growth of the Conception of God," page 111.

[18]See "Philosophy of Religion," Vol. 1, pages 96, 105, 106,
155, 156.

[19]"History of Religions," Vol. I, page 346.

[20]"Philosophy of Religion," Vol. I, page 97.

the services expected of it, it is torn from its temple and flung into the mud." Fritz Schultze observes:

The Neapolitans once called Saint Gennaro *vecchio, ladrone, birbone, scelerato,* because he had not checked a stream of lava. Some Spanish peasants during a protracted drought threw the Virgin into a pond, and called her witch, wench, etc. . . . To this day Russian peasants whip saints' images; to this day images of the Virgin are put in prison by Italian peasants precisely as the negro does with his fetishes, when he would punish them or keep them from harming him.[21]

One of the commonest of practices in Mexico is to punish the saints' images just as a very cruel parent would punish a disobedient child—by exposing them to storms, rains, winds, the hot sun, etc. They also show them contempt by withholding from them ordinary reverence. In China the gods are held responsible and sometimes punished for failure to send rain, or for sending too much rain.

The "high-brows" among both heathen and Romanists claim to use the images only as symbols. The difficulty about that is that the most ignorant, who most need such aids to the imagination, are the ones who fail to use them for that purpose. Why should intelligent people require so much help? But if they do need it in order to adore the saints, why should they not also need an image of the Almighty? Neither official heathenism nor official Romanism recognizes such use of images. If the symbolic use of images is sanctioned by Holy Writ, then all we have to do is to enlighten the heathen so that they will all be clever enough to use them in that way. If all Catholics could be educated suf-

---

[21] "Fetichism," page 63.

ficiently to denounce their theologians who have
ignorantly taught that the image is a resting place
for the saint, the Catholic Church might still be
saved from much gross superstition.

2. *Rome's ideas of the other world and the future life
are pagan.*

(1) Purgatory is based on the heathen doctrine of
penance. Indulgences which may be secured by
money paid to the priest for masses is not merely an
extension of the idea of penance; it is a trick by means
of which the clergy make merchandise of the ignorant and superstitious.

The so-called sins for which one must go to purgatory are not so much real delinquencies as disobedience to the priest or neglect of ceremonies.

The kind of suffering, undergone by careless or
negligent or disobedient Catholics, in purgatory is
indescribable; only a heathen god could be guilty of
castigating human beings in such a way for such
faults. The most intense fire to be endured day and
night for great periods of time is held to be the methods employed by the Catholic god for the purification of those who die in grace and who have yet some
faults to expiate. And the folly of it is that no sort of
repentance is possible or could be efficacious in
purifying a soul in purgatory.

The means by which a soul is delivered from that
awful place is the old heathen one of favoritism; all
depends upon the amount of influence the sinner may
have among his earthly relatives, friends, and
benefactors.

(2) The Catholic hell is a farce; it, too, is a reproduction of heathenism.

While Romish theologians do hold that men sometimes go to hell for real sins, yet it is usually the best people who are permitted by the priests to go there.

DEEDS FOR WHICH PEOPLE ARE SUPPOSED BY ROMANISTS TO GO TO HELL

1. Sending their children to a public school.
2. Being married without a priest.
3. Reading a Protestant Bible without permission.
4. Taking part in a Protestant ceremony.
5. Attending regularly Protestant Church services.
6. Voting in a political election contrary to the priest's command.
7. Supporting, as a principle, the doctrine of the separation of Church and State.
8. Favoring the doctrine of freedom of worship for Protestants.
9. Refusing to boycott a heretic.
10. Refusing to break faith with a heretic in order to denounce him secretly to the Iniquisitors or other Church authorities.
11. Taking a bona fide oath to support a government which does not recognize the Roman Church.
12. Reading a book which has been prohibited by the Catholic Church.
13. Joining a Protestant Church.
14. Refusing to "condemn, reject, and anathematize" those Protestant doctrines which are contrary to Romanism.
15. Examining those doctrines which they are bound to anathematize.
16. Denouncing publicly the Catholic doctrines of theft and gambling.

If a Catholic is determined to go to hell, the quickest and most certain way to do it is to live a correct life, walking in all the commandments of the Lord blameless.

(3) *Limbus patrum* is the place where good men went who died before the Christian era. That seems to be a revival of the vague pagan idea of the place of the shades for those who died in those days.

(4) Heaven is the place where good Catholics and invincibly ignorant non-Catholics go.

An examination of the conditions on which men go to hell will reveal the fact that according to Romanism one has to be intensely wicked and unpatriotic in order to be admitted by the Romish Saint Peter into the glory world. While priests, by keeping their people in ignorance of the most vital parts of their system, are able to retain some good people in their Church, yet the genuine Romanist goes to heaven for his loyalty to his Church, not because of his faith in God.

The Romish theory makes it impossible for Protestants to be saved except on condition that they live much better lives than Catholics do. The doctrine that perfect repentance (contrition) is necessary for a Protestant to be forgiven, while imperfect repentance (attrition) is sufficient for a Catholic, can be explained only on the ground that morality is not primary in Romanism.

Salvation by magic makes Bible-reading of small consequence; it minimizes right living; it depreciates education except for the priests and their fanatical defenders; it emasculates statesmanship; it subordinates science to sacerdotal philosophy; it divorces the ethics of business from the authority of religion; it saps the foundation of spirituality among both priests and people; it turns Sunday into a holiday (magic can be performed by the priest in a very short time and is a substitute for thought); it delivers the laity into the hand of their (non-)spiritual guides; it turns heaven into a receptacle for blind devotees of Papalism, and it shuts its gates on the purest and noblest of the human race.

(5) *Limbus infantum,* where unbaptized infants are supposed to go, is purely pagan. For the accident of not being baptized an innocent babe is maliciously consigned to a place where it will never see the face of God. Some humane Romish theologians contend that it is better off than it would be if it were simply dead and wiped out of existence, but others just as high up in the hierarchy describe its condition in a way to make rocks weep—unless the rocks knew that it was all a joke. Very probably the priests generally do not believe it, but it is a very remunerative doctrine. The leaders claim that they do not charge for baptizing an infant; they only expect a donation, but the humble faithful Catholics know that if the voluntary gift is not forthcoming the helpless child of their heart must be cut off from God and heaven and from the company of its baptized parents throughout the ceaseless ages of eternity. Unless the baptism has the magical power of making the child purer and better, then it has the power of moving the heart of the Romish chief god, or else it operates in a realm of forces over which the gods do not or cannot have control.

3. *The Catholic idea of the deposit of revelation is pagan.*

We may grasp at once the preponderance of paganism with reference to revelation by reflecting on the great mass of tradition as compared to the volume of

7

Biblical lore, covering only about one thousand pages. The Romish notion of the sources of authority in morals and dogma is that they are to be found in the Bible and tradition. In order to make a priesthood still more necessary than it already is, the hierarchy keep the tradition in a vague form. Should the Spirit of God suddenly move upon the face of this pagan world, which thus far has been without form and void, and if God should once more say, "Let there be light," papal priests would call for the rocks and mountains to fall on them and hide them from the face of him that sitteth on the throne. Just that will happen one of these days.

The Rig-Veda of the Hindus was peculiarly the property of the priesthood.

While Homer's "Iliad" was not technically kept in the hands of the priests only, it was practically the possession mainly of the learned to be interpreted allegorically by them.

The Confucian philosophy was for the same reason the special property of the learned and the leisure class.

The Avesta of the Zoroastrians allowed one of its four parts to be used as a book of private devotion by the laity; the other three portions—and they constitute the most of the book—were mainly liturgical and were to be read and used by the priests.

The Book of the Dead consists of a lot of magical material which mainly represents the beliefs of Egyptian priests. The cults of Egypt were primarily priestly; the formulæ were necessarily for their guidance.

Among savages, who have little or no written language, the divine revelation must be kept in the memory, but by the priests.

In all cases these various so-called divine revelations contain great masses of stuff very similar to the written traditions of Rome, and the services of a magically ordained clergy must be engaged to explain enough of it to pacify the laity and make them believe that they have a right to understand a few of the religious secrets.

The unwritten traditions of Rome, if there are any at this last date, are entirely in the hands of the hierarchy.

All this effectually ties the hands of the laity; the task is too great for the busy man to master. More yet; since the Bible must be made to harmonize with all this rubbish, only he who is familiar with both the Bible and tradition can comprehend either. It follows that the Protestant ministry is disqualified to expound Scripture; of course all laymen, Catholic and Protestant, are unfit for so complicated a piece of work.

4. *Magic is at the very base of all Romanism and all other forms of heathenism.*

This may be divided into two parts: *Ceremonialism;* that is, the doctrine that material things— sound, gesticulations, intonations, words, vestments, colors, etc.—carry grace in and of themselves, and *legalism*, which is an improvement upon ceremonies, but which makes salvation depend upon certain deeds and words which comply with prescribed rules of conduct.

That things which are essentially unmoral are held to be fraught with spiritual energy is absurd and

baleful. Bosman declares that "certain negroes of
Guinea imagine that when they cross the river of
death they are questioned by a superhuman being,
who asks them if they have observed the sacred days
and if they have abstained from prohibited kinds of
food."[22]

Romanism makes abstinence from meat on Friday
as important as any moral precept; to refuse deliberately to abstain, without an excuse or a dispensation, would be to merit hell fire.

Protection, by *exorcism*, against demons is universal among those of animistic faiths—*i. e.*, savages.
It penetrates all those religions which are simply
polytheistic, as, *e. g.*, the early Chinese, the Teutons,
etc.; it saturates the idolatrous religions everywhere;
it even finds a place in Mohammedanism, an ostensi-
bly monotheistic faith. It was also practiced among
the Jews, whose religion was based on an ethical
supreme Being. If it is contended that the practice
of Jesus in driving out demons sanctions Romish,
pagan, and savage mummery, I answer, Jesus did all
his marvelous works by virtue of his *personal righteousness* and his communion with God, while *Catholic priests insist that their power does not depend on
their righteousness at all, but purely on the Sacrament
of Order*.

Frantic feasts are practically universal among
savages, pagans, and Catholics. The Lenten season
came from the Teutons. That non-Christian religions are mainly based on emotion and therefore in-
duce to frenzied and dissipating feasts is so well
known that it hardly needs to be more than men-

---

[22]"Growth of the Conception of God," page 193.

tioned. An instance of this practice by Romanists is shown in an account, written by Lilian T. Mowrer in the *Kansas City Times* of June 11, 1919, of a Catholic miracle in Italy. She states: "At the church of Santa Chiara last night [she writes from Naples under date of May 4] at 9:20 o'clock, the blood of Saint Januarius, a sacred relic preserved for nearly sixteen centuries, changed from its dry, powdered state into a rich, red fluid, thereby proving the ever-watchful interest that the patron saint of Naples takes in the thousands of pious Neapolitans who come to witness the triennial miracle." A long account is given of this so-called miracle; how the descendants of Neapolitans who were contemporaries of the saint could pray in such way as to cause his blood to liquefy; how they worked themselves up into a hysterical state; how the church was full of excited people; how the prayers and chants continued until the results were secured.

Penance is another form of ceremonialism; purgatory is the extension of this balderdash to a future state of existence. That one may or must pay for his sins in suffering is essentially heathen. That self-inflicted pain in this life, or that the flames of purgatory in the next, can purify the soul is contrary to all the facts we can gather. We find that people are not made better because of suffering. Those forms of affliction which come to us in the providence of God may be made the occasion of our repentance. The sufferings which we bring upon ourselves deliberately in order to please a contemptible deity are an affront to the Christian's God. Penance and purgatory may have originated with the Zoroastrians and Buddhists, for both held these two doctrines long before they became a part of Romanism.

5. *The priesthood of Romanism retains all its heathen characteristics.*

In Romanism this pagan element is much more powerful and dangerous than it ever was among the heathen. Priests have always been noted for their secrecy, avarice, cunning, tendency to profligacy, ambition, pretense to magical power, unscrupulous control of the masses, intense hatred of rivals, and affected sanctity.

Priestly control of devoted women and resistance of ethical religions through these fanatical women have always been practiced just as they are now by Catholic priests. Under priestly influence, the Jews urged on the devout women of honorable estate against Paul and Barnabas. "The priests in India, and the women who are there, and everywhere, most subject to priestly influence, are to-day the principal opponents of religious change and of social and economic advancement."[23]

The various methods used by the priestly class to exalt itself above the common people are all heathen in origin. Celibacy is Buddhistic; as also is the tonsure. The Zoroastrians used a dead language in their ritual; they also called a priest to hear confessions and administer extreme unction just before death. Buddhist priests hear confessions semi-monthly. Holy vestments came from pagan Rome and originally from Egypt. Professor Ladd finds the peculiar power of the priests to consist in his control over the occult. Says he:

---

[23]"Philosophy of Religion," Vol. I, page 405.

Among the Redskins, the Africans, and the Australians we find magic and religion existing together. . . . In China to-day we have in Taoism a most impressive example of the degrading side of Spiritism, for it is the incessant and depressing dread of invisible, superhuman spirits which gives to the Taoist priests, or "yellow tops," their power over the people. Nor is this power, in its origin and character, essentially different from that which the peasant women in certain parts of France attribute to their Christian [Catholic] priests, and believe them to exercise over the elements by certain mystical prayers. In this respect, as Roskoff well says, "There is no essential difference between the Siberian Shaman and the North American medicine man, the South American Paye, the South African Mganga, the Australian sorcerer, and him on the Islands of the South Seas;" and we might add, the Taoist and Christian [Catholic] priest, on every occasion that he lends himself to the practice of magic."[24]

Catholic priests are not alone in having a corner on purgatory. In China "the souls of the departed are believed to gain release from hell only through the prayers of the priest, for which he receives a good fee."[25]

In Latin America thinking men generally do not allow their wives and daughters to attend the confessional, because it is personally either dangerous or shocking, also because priests meddle with political affairs. Early Buddhist instructions were to the effect that priests must not look at women and should, if possible, avoid speaking to them. Barton observes that "the Buddhistic order of monks tended to loose the bond of the family and of the State." Liguori, the great Catholic theologian, advises the clergy to be extremely careful in confess-

---

[24]"Philosophy of Religion," Vol. I, pages 103, 104.
[25]"Religions of the World," Barton, page 218.

ing women and gives the strictest rules for their guidance. He states that such confession is the most dangerous thing a priest can do and adds that many have fallen on account of it.[26]

Buddhist priests in Japan in the thirteenth century were guilty of having concubines; the same is true of Catholic priests in South America in the nineteenth and twentieth centuries, and in Europe from the eleventh to the sixteenth centuries. By having their own concubines and by extracting those secrets from the wife which she should confess only to her husband, Romish priests "loose the bonds of the family." By mixing in politics and directing their penitents how to vote they "loose the bonds of the State."

6. *An inferior moral code is the vortex into which all magical religions inevitably flow.* This has been the uniform result in all heathen cults; it has been precisely the same with Romanism. No sooner are morals degraded than those cults come to be despised.

The Egyptians allowed a considerable amount of magic and virtually permitted morals to become secondary.

In Hinduism "the account of merit and demerit of a devotee is balanced up to the last moment, including on the credit side his religious devotion and observances—the latter taken at an extravagant valuation compared with moral derelictions. The rites performed by his relatives after his death are also imputed to him as merit."[27] All this is true also of Buddhism.

---

[26] "Roman Catholicism Analyzed," pages 94, 96.
[27] "History of Religions," Vol. I, page 359.

With the Babylonians ethics was required, but "the main effort was to appease the divine anger, so as to remove the affliction."

In Buddhism the Sangha order has four great requirements dealing with morals; then follow thirteen that deal with formalities relating to cleanness and uncleanness, the way to build huts, the use of robes, rags, bowls, etc.

Zoroastrianism degenerated in its later stages. "Morals are in the later Avesta part of a sacred law, and that law includes in the same categories and under the same sanctions much that is not intrinsically moral at all, or to which religion gives fictitious moral values. Ritual correctness, ceremonial purity, sacerdotal casuistry are raised to the dignity of moral obligations."

The Cretans made a lasting contribution to the Roman Catholic religion when they gave it the two famous qualities of lying and avarice. We must not believe that the Cretans invented those two sins; nor shall we contend that the Roman Catholic cult would have lacked at these points had they not known the Cretans. But the peculiar eminence of Romish priests as deceivers and money-grubbers deserves a unique explanation.

7. *Conflict with civil government and the death penalty came from various pagan sources, but it was left for Romanism to carry them forward to their highest point of development.* Union of Church and State was intrinsic in the Semitic faiths.[28] They taught

---

[28]"Religion of the Semites," W. Robertson Smith, pages 20, 21.

that one was born into the State and it was criminal
to investigate the grounds of his faith. This is the
constant appeal made by priests to their members in
Romish countries. "The religion of our fathers" is
the talisman to close eyes, ears, mouth, and reason.
"We shall see nothing, hear nothing, discuss nothing,
know nothing," is the motto of Catholic "beatos"
(blessed ones). Church and State cannot be perfectly united until the emperor is deified. The
typical results of this *régime* are seen in China, Japan,
Turkey, Spain, Italy, Bolivia, and Austria. Recognition of the divinity of the emperor, as in Japan,
China, and pagan Rome; acceptance of papal infallibility and supremacy in modern Rome; submission
to the inerrancy and secular dominion of Mohammed
and his caliphs, all amount to the same thing. They
are all pagan, blasphemous, ridiculous, and deadly.

The persecution of heretics is a logical consequence
of the union of Church and State. Christianity
makes no provision for the imprisonment or murder
of heretics. Jesus undertook nothing of the kind and
laid down no rule or principle for it. The idiotic interpretation of the "two swords" employed by Pope
Boniface VIII. in his bull, Unam Sanctam, is clear
evidence that Rome can find nothing in Scripture to
warrant her dominion over civil government. Boniface explains that when Jesus said to his disciples
that the two swords which they carried with them the
night before his death were *enough*, he meant that
the Roman Catholic Church should have *two swords*
and that these two swords meant temporal and spiritual power. If the New Testament really sanctioned
the unholy union between Church and State which is

claimed by Romanists, some passage could be found that actually taught it. The "two swords" argument is unworthy of the veriest ignoramus.

When we consider the character of pagan religions we can easily see that union of Church and State must be effected, else reasonable men will laugh their magical pretensions out of court. What sensible man would be willing to pay taxes to an institution whose foundation rested on the efficacy of hocus-pocus and a priestly caste to keep luckless souls from frying in white-hot fires? Since the best men in the country are to be subdued by sacerdotal humbugs, it will have to be done through fanatics and by the powerful arguments of prison cells and firing squads.

When we sing,

> "Faith of our fathers! living still
> In spite of dungeon, fire, and sword,"

let us not deceive ourselves. It was not our Roman Catholic fathers who were persecuted for their faith in Christ. From righteous Abel to Jeremiah, and to Jesus Christ, ungodly men have persistently persecuted the people of God. The Romish Church has always, where it was possible, persecuted the same sort of people who were sawn asunder, burned, and exiled by pagan Rome. The martyrs executed by the Catholic Church were Christians who insisted on practicing and preaching the faith of Christ, of the apostles, of the early Church, and of modern Protestants. The Romish Church has often suffered, but seldom has she herself been persecuted. She has been resisted, punished, suppressed, and denounced for her intrigue and her authorized iniquities.

Vicente de la Fuente, in his "Plurality of Religions," reveals a remarkable solicitude to prove that the intolerance of Romanism is exactly like that of other pagan cults. Says he:

Of the intolerance of ancient peoples the Abbe, Bergier in his "Historical and Dogmatic Treatise on the True Religion," . . . shows that the Greeks were intolerant in religious matters. To prove it he adduces the doctrine of Carondas and Zaleuco in their Codes, of Pythagoras in his school and of Plato in Book X. of his laws. The execution of Socrates, the decree of death against Alcibiades for having blasphemed the mysteries of Ceres, the condemnation of Diagoras for atheism, and of Theodore, who was condemned by the Areopagus for the same cause, the persecutions of Anaxagoras Estilpon, and of the celebrated Aspasia, accused of impiety, show that the Greeks, in the epoch of their greatest culture, wisdom, and glory, although polytheistic, were not tolerant, and persecuted with capital punishment atheism, rationalism, impiety, and blasphemy.

As to Rome, her religious intolerance before and after the Empire is well known. The law of the Twelve Tables prohibited the introduction of strange rites and gods without the approbation of the magistrates; but, according to Dionysius of Halicarnasus, no strange rite was admitted to Rome by public authority, as was done in other places. Cicero, in his work "*De Legibus*," showed himself exceedingly intolerant, considering disobedience to the pontifices and the augurs as a capital crime, dating this severe restriction to the times of Numa Pompilius. . . . Their practice was also in accordance with their doctrine. In the year 345 the magistrates were charged to watch lest any new cult should be introduced into Rome.

We may add that the same Bergier in his "*Diccionario de Teologia*," article on "*Tolerancia*," contends that Romanism should control the State. After citing Plato in favor of persecution of dissident religions, he answers the objection that religion in general should be supported. Says he: "A religion thus understood is nothing more than irreligion." It must be intolerance toward all other than the established organized religion, and that such religion must be the Roman Catholic. His appeal to heathen kings and governments is natural; his insistence that religion in general is useless is in accord with the whole philosophy of Romanism both pagan and so-called Christian.

If the characteristics we have examined were incidental, or even of secondary importance, we might regard them as mere "heathen survivals" in a higher religion; but they are virtually all there is to Romanism and paganism. If Romanism has a bad chief deity, with his lesser gods, a great goddess, and images, all just as the heathen have them, she is pagan at heart. If Romanism teaches and practices magic as the essential part of her spiritual and moral life, she is certainly pagan. If the priesthood of the Catholic Church functions without regard to its moral character and has the same traits that are found among the heathen, then Rome has another indelible mark of pagan nature.

After we have shown the basic qualities of Romanism, we shall give a concise account of the essential immorality that must always come from a trifling god at the head of a pantheon, a religion whose warp and woof is ceremonial buncombe, and a cult which relies on a priesthood for its efficacy. These result in the destruction of morality, the weakening of civil government, and finally the collapse of entire nations.

THE TEUTONIC CONTRIBUTION OF PAGAN ELEMENTS TO ROMANISM[29]

In addition to these fundamental practices and beliefs, which came directly from the Semitic, Egyptian, Zoroastrian, Ægean, Greek, and Roman religions, certain elements from the Teutonic faiths had a molding influence on Romanism. I shall not enter into detail here; the reader is urged to read Saussaye's great work. Some Teutonic elements that have influenced Romanism are as follows:

The sign of the cross, which was probably evolved from the hammer of Thor.

Magical formulæ.

Sword banquets. These bring to mind the famous bull, *Unam Sanctam*, where Boniface VIII. argues for the two swords.

Innumerable saints.

The burning of lights near the corpse to keep evil spirits, or the soul itself, at a distance.

Divinities and semi-divinities—*e. g.*, norms, swan-maidens, etc.

Boisterous funeral banquets, progenitors of Irish Catholic wakes.

Multiplicity of bodies of departed divinities. The Catholic hierarchy does not blush to show the craniums of the same saint in a half dozen places at once. One of these phenomena was once explained by a zealous devotee as the cranium of a certain saint first while he was a boy and then after he became a man. After such an exposition the faithful could readily comprehend why one of the skulls should be so much smaller than the other.

Processions carrying images.

It may be noted in passing that the Teutons were

[29]"Religion of the Teutons," P. D. Chantepie de la Saussaye.

in harmony with all the seven elements of Romanism and of all other pagan cults, but their specific contributions were mainly of two sorts—namely, that of certain species of polytheism and of magic.

THE FAMILY LIKENESS BETWEEN ROMANISM AND THE RELIGIONS OF AMERICAN ABORIGINES [30]

It is remarkable that the early settlers in America should have found virtually the same religion that had struggled against Christianity in Europe for fifteen centuries. It illustrates the solidarity of paganism resulting from the unity of the human mind as expressed in the various nature religions which men have developed in widely separated ages and climes.

1. An imperfect chief deity, worshiped without images, lesser gods, a great goddess, images used in the cult of the smaller gods.

(1) The Great Spirit of the Redskins is well known as an invisible great god. The Incas of Peru had some such god who was superior to all phenomena. "A temple was constructed in a vale by the sea near Callao, wherein his worship was to be conducted without images or human sacrifices."

(2) The aborigines of both Americas had, in addition to their more or less vague highest god, their pantheons of smaller deities of various ranks.

(3) There were a great goddess and numerous female deities.

The goddess, Tonantzin, Our Dear Mother, was the most widely loved of Nahuatl divinities, and it is because her mantle

---

[30] "The Native Religions of Mexico and Peru," Reville; "The Myths of the New World," Brinton.

fell upon Our Lady of Guadalupe that the latter now can boast of the most popular shrine in Mexico. When Cortez first explored Acalan, the modern Tabasco, he found the chief temple of their greatest town dedicated to a goddess, not to a god; and the Isla de las Mugeres, off the coast of Yucatan, was so named because all its fanes were sacred to female deities.[31]

(4) Images were used in great profusion. It is remarkable what a vast variety of these one can see in the national museum in Mexico City, especially when we consider that Romish priests destroyed so many of them.

(5) While these images ordinarily merely furnished a home for their gods, the Aztecs also had the same habit practiced by Romanists—that is, of eating the god.

2. A heaven for the "faithful," and from which the unfaithful were excluded for ritualistic faults rather than for want of moral character.

3. Tradition as the basis for priestly and religious authority.

4. Magic universally practiced. There were great and solemn ceremonies practiced at birth, marriage, and death. They had holy water and baptism for magical purposes. Exorcism was common. As was to be expected, they had hysterical feasts in due heathen style. There was also penance. The penitentes of New Mexico punish themselves even to crucifixion; they are good Catholics and also good heathen, as is shown not only by their fanaticism, but in the fact that they are ready to murder any intruder and then lie about it to shield themselves from

---

[31]"Myths of the New World," pages 178, 179.

the courts. Are they not defending their religion? That is good Romanism.

5. A priesthood, with pagan prerogatives. There was the sacrament of order which inducted these men into their priestly office. There were convents with monks and nuns; also hermits who lived austerely in the desert. Those priests had the power, prestige, exclusiveness, secrecy, and intolerance common to all heathen priesthoods. They used magic, worshiped in an unknown tongue, and had a grave and solemn countenance and dignified step. There were the practice of confession of sins and priestly absolution.

6. A feeble effort to unite piety and morals to the detriment of the latter.

7. Union of Church and State, and submission of all people to the high priest, Pontifex Maximus. This was a Mexican custom. There was a similar absolutism under the Incas of Peru.

The persecution of dissenters. Roman sacrifice was an Aztec practice. It was little less diabolical than the Catholic Inquisition. In each case it was done to please the gods, in the name of religion, during and just following the Middle Ages; in each case it was abandoned under pressure of a higher civilization resulting from the Protestant Reformation. The Romish Inquisition in Latin America superseded the original pagan practice. The papal system of propaganda had some advantages over the indigenous sort; it employed a more exquisite torture; it showed a more pious solicitude for the eternal fate of the victim; it was more thorough in the discovery of heretics.

The usual collapse of nations, governments, and

8

tribes followed there as it has in other pagan and Catholic countries.

RESEMBLANCES BETWEEN ROMANISM AND BUDDHISM

My friend Dr. M. C. Wilcox, who is familiar with the philosophies of both Buddhism and Romanism, has kindly furnished me with the following description of a religion which was founded more than five hundred years before Augustus Cæsar was declared Pontifex Maximus, and about nine hundred years before the Religion of the Cæsars became the so-called Christian Church. The Doctor does not seek to prove that Romanism borrowed from Buddhism, but that they both sprang from the same human source.

The similarity of many of the forms and ceremonies of Buddhism to those of the Church of Rome has not escaped attention. Early Roman Catholic missionaries tried to account for undeniable resemblances by the supposition that Satan had counterfeited "Mother Church" in order to preoccupy the minds of the people with the false to the exclusion of the true. But every student of religions accounts for the similarities by the indisputable solidarity of paganism, ancient and modern.

Many are the points of resemblance: Each religion—Roanism and Buddhism—has its supreme head, the pope at Rome with his cardinals and the pope, or Grand Lama, and cardinals of Tibetan Lamaism—a form of Buddhism. (The Grand Lama, as is well known, reigns in barbaric grandeur at Lassa, the capital of Tibet. He is considered immortal, for when he dies his soul is supposed to pass into the body of some infant whom the priests claim to identify by certain signs and who is taught that the same spirit that animated the body of his predecessor dwells within himself.)

Romanism and Buddhism also both have an unmarried priesthood; monasteries and nunneries; prayers in an unknown tongue; prayers to saints and other intercessors, especially to a virgin—the Goddess of Mercy—with a child; prayers for the dead; endless repetition of prayers, with the use of a rosary; works of merit and supererogation; self-imposed austerities and bodily inflictions; formal daily services consisting of chants, burning of candles, sprinkling of holy water, bowings, prostrations, marchings, countermarchings, etc. Both systems have fast days and feast days, religious processions, images, pictures, and fabulous legends; and both revere and worship relics, real and pretended. Pagodas, for example, are built as mementos of a piece of bone, a tooth, or a finger nail, etc., of Buddha, just as Roman Catholic cathedrals are supposed to be rendered more sacred by wood from the "True Cross" and by relics of the saints.

One who is familiar with the worship of both these cults can hardly decide which is the more heathenish. Compare by way of illustration the regular Romish service with the worship in a Buddhist temple:

The regular morning and evening ritual is chanted in connection with the burning of incense, the beating of drums, bells, etc. The whole exercise lasts about an hour. As a rule that which the priests chant is a crude imitation of the words of the original Pali as represented by Chinese characters and, of course, is utterly meaningless. But, as is true of the Romish priests and the Latin service, the priests of Buddhism attach great importance to the confused jumble because Pali is the sacred language of the birthplace of Gautama and is therefore of divine origin and efficacy.

In large Buddhist temples are long rows of kneeling stools upon which are placed straw hassocks. The monks stand behind these stools and intone the prescribed ritual. An abbot, as master of ceremonies, conducts the service, signaling when to bow, kneel, fall prostrate, rise again, etc. The murmur of the constant chant is accompanied by intermittent music (?) from instruments that the Oriental loves and the Occidental execrates. From time to time an acolyte beats a drum, another tinkles a bell, and now and then there breaks in the discordant clangor of an immense gong.

After a while a fresh note is struck and, at a certain signal, the priests—sometimes several hundred in number—separate into two companies and for a long time wind in and out in a slow and solemn procession.   Backward and forward with measured tread they pace along, their hands clasped, their heads bowed, their lips still murmuring the same unintelligible refrain, Ah-Mi-Ta-Fu, Ah-Mi-Ta-Fu, a title of Buddha, the repetition of which many thousands of times is supposed to be as replete with merit as the repetition of Paternosters by Romanists.[32]

Legalism is slightly better than ceremonialism and is usually inseparably joined with it.   Not only do Romanists and pagans have a multitude of details which must be observed, but savages are under the same burden.   Everything in the life of a savage is prescribed in detail.   The masses of the Chinese are not free from it; perhaps partly on account of the animism of their uncivilized ancestors, and yet it is inherent in the higher religions there.

Legalism was a stepping-stone with the Jews toward a spiritual religion.   It became, however, with the majority of that people a permanent wayside station.   There they have stood in a state of arrested development for nineteen centuries.

---

[32]Excerpts from a lecture on Buddhism, delivered at Garrett Biblical Institute, Evanston, Ill., by M. C. Wilcox, Ph.D.

CHAPTER IV

THE PAGAN EVOLUTION OF ROMANISM

1. THE PRE-CHRISTIAN PERIOD (650? B.C. TO 27 B.C.—623 YEARS)

THE Roman Catholic Church, in its present character (1924), is about one thousand nine hundred and fifty years old. The six centuries in which the religion of ancient Rome was being developed were years in which the seven vital elements of all pagan religions were becoming solidified.

Beginning with the ancient simple cult of the Latins, which was affected considerably by the primitive religious notions of the Sabines, the old Roman system was gradually modified and developed for six or seven centuries. This we shall call the pre-Christian period.

While we know little of the Etruscans, it appears certain that they exercised a powerful influence in leading Romans into their remarkable ambition for world-control. That which Romanists call their Christian "note" of universality is not Christian at all; it is the old pagan idea of conquest. The Etruscans were intelligent, vigorous, commercial, warlike, powerful, ambitious. They built massive walls and strong towers, they lived off of the labor of the poor, they based their power on religion. These three items Rome absorbed and has never relinquished. Coming between the rise of the city-state and the influence of the Greeks, these Etruscans stamp their indelible mark of aggressiveness on the Romans.

(117)

Assyrians, Babylonians, Egyptians, Zoroastrians, Buddhists, Ægeans, Cretans, and Greeks all contributed to the greatest empire the world had ever seen. The pagan concepts of all these peoples were focused in the city of Rome in large measure by the year 27 B.C., when Augustus Cæsar reorganized the religion of the empire. Our study of the contributions of these various religions to the Italian religion has been in the main an examination of the pre-Christian period of the Catholic religion.

The two indispensable heathen elements—to wit, ritual and force—found their place in Pagan Romanism when the Emperor became the head of the religion of the reorganized State as Pontifex Maximus. The etymology of the word "pontiff" (Umbrian *puntes*, pl., probably meaning some religious rites in sacrificing) indicates that his religious power consisted in magic. Being already at the head of the soldiery and all other governmental forms of force, Cæsar was a perfect pagan ruler when he made subordination to ritual a test of citizenship.

2. The Parallel Period (27 B.C. to 380 A.D.— 407 Years)

We may ignore the fifty-six years between the elevation of Augustus to the sublime height of Pontifex Maximus and Emperor-god (27 B.C.) to the death of Jesus Christ (29 A.D.) by making it a part of the parallel period, for the Roman religion was getting ready unconsciously for the great struggle in which the victory fell officially to pagan Rome.

From the time of Jesus's ministry, ending in the year 29 A.D., down to the year 380 A.D., the original

Roman Catholic Church (known then as the Religion of the Empire) ran parallel to Christianity. This can be demonstrated by showing that the ubiquitous pagan features of ritual and brute force have been essential in the same way: (1) in the religion of Pagan Rome before the Christian era; (2) in the religion of the Roman Empire during this period; (3) since the metamorphosis of pagan Romanism and its reappearance under the name of Roman Catholic Christianity. It was impossible for the religion of Christ to syncretize with heathenism. Two kinds of food may be properly mixed; two poisons may be combined; but a mixture of equal parts of food and poison is not a compromise; it is a surrender of food to poison. When early Christianity undertook to blend with paganism, the product was not a mixture; it was simple heathenism. Christianity is unique; it is founded on the person of Him who had no fault in him. The spirit and letter of the law of Christ are completely at variance with the essence of heathenism. The ceremonies which Jesus recommended were baptism and the Lord's Supper; practically nothing was said as to the details of their administration. Jesus announced plainly that his kingdom was not of this world. He would not take the sword in his own defense. The New Testament gives no warrant for the temporal supremacy of the gospel ministry.

From 380 to the Reformation those sects which continued to follow the system of Christ asserted the spiritual nature of the kingdom of God in the world. After the Reformation, such large numbers turned away from Rome that the movement was not thoroughly Christian; they had been so contaminated by contact with the heathenism of the Middle Ages that they continued for a time to practice it. The germ of the Reformation was the spiritual nature of the Church; this was worked out more thoroughly in certain countries where Christianity came more fully into its own.

The differences between the religion of the Empire during the four first centuries of the Christian era and the so-called Christian Church which followed are only superficial; the principles are identical. After her change of name paganism became more thoroughly organized and developed a more elaborate philosophy than was ever realized by Greeks or Romans. There are certain marks of identity—*e. g.*, (1) the same center, Rome; (2) the same name given to the heads of each system, Pontifex Maximus; (3) the same language, the Latin; (4) the same priestly paraphernalia; (5) the same method—*i. e.*, "divide and conquer;" (6) outward conformity to law; (7) the same organization; (8) punishment of dissenters. It might be possible for the Catholic Church to have all these as simply an inheritance. But if it is shown that the content in each case is at heart just what it was in pagan Romanism, we cannot escape the conclusion that the two epochs are different from each other only in name. From Rome as a center there went out in the first four centuries the authority to persecute Christians; so it was that Rome launched her murderous assault against Christians after she was supposed to be the center of Christianity. Pontifex Maximus was as much a title of blood after the Romish pope assumed it as it ever was before, and he murdered his victims for the same delinquencies—

that is, ritualistic faults and the crime of thinking for oneself. The Latin language (it later became an unknown tongue and as such fell under the rebuke of the Apostle Paul) was the language of paganism and, while used temporarily as a vehicle for the Holy Scriptures, it is yet the language selected by Catholic theologians as peculiarly useful for the preservation of the rottenness of filthy discussions regarding the confessional and especially to express formulæ of exorcism. Both the obscenities of the confessional and the nonsense of exorcism are pagan. Priestly garbs are supposed to have magical power. The original heathen brutality is very evident in Romanism now as to her methods and organization; she is an absolute monarchy now as always and fights her opponents in the same old pagan way.

In tracing the genealogy of Romanism back to Augustus Cæsar rather than to Peter or to Jesus Christ, we do not forget that certain pagan elements did creep into the early Christian Church and that the preparation for surrender was gradual. But this did not make the early Church really pagan; it was Christian at heart. The nature of a religion must be determined by its deep vital principles and not by its accretions. Before 380 the religion which Jesus founded was truly Christian despite its trend toward ritualism and the persecution of the heathen who surrounded it. But when official Christianity abandoned the principles of its Founder it became at once truly pagan.

The two lines of development have continued to the present time side by side. The Christian religion began with Christ; it was contaminated by heathenism for about four centuries; it passed through the awful persecutions of the Middle Ages, having for its great enemy the Roman Catholic Church; it flourished again at the Reformation; it came into its own during the nineteenth and twentieth centuries; it is now entering a new era in which it is about to declare its eternal severance from its old enemy.

The Roman Catholic Church began in pagan Rome before Christ; it grappled with Christianity for nearly four hundred years; it calmly changed its name in 380 to that of Catholic Christianity, leaving the Christian Church to be called by whatever names might be conferred upon it. After trying in vain for more than a millennium to crush its rival: it crystallized into present-day Romanism.

Now we have two distinct religions: Christianity, which began with Christ, A.D. 29, and which is, therefore (1924), one thousand eight hundred and ninety-five years old (unless we prefer to trace it from the reputed date of the birth of Christ, which would make it one thousand nine hundred and twenty-four years old); and Romanism, which began officially with Augustus Cæsar, 27 B.C., and which is now one thousand nine hundred and fifty-one years old.

Jesus denounced with withering scorn Pharisees, scribes, and other Jewish leaders, because they had forsaken and were misrepresenting the religion which they were supposed to represent—that is, the religion of Abraham, of Moses, and of the prophets. This does not warrant us in condemning Catholic priests for degrading the religion of Christ; they have not degraded it. Rather are we to follow the method of

Jesus with the Samaritans, if possible. He did not accuse them of apostasy; he stated plainly that salvation was of the Jews. The Samaritan was originally a different cult from that of the Bible. We must, however, rebuke Romish priests for their pretense to Christianity and their usurpation of Christian leadership.

Our task is not to recall, but to call Catholics to the religion of Christ. We may be sure that there are Good Samaritans who practice Christian virtues; these need to be recognized and encouraged. But to compromise with idolatry—either Romish or pagan—is a sin. Protestantism is suffering untold harm to-day because many of her leaders teach that Romanism and evangelical Christianity are at heart the same religion.

It is true that the Catholic Church has never been able to prevent some Christians from entering or remaining within her fold. There are members of the Catholic Church who do not wish to extirpate or kill heretics and who would dare to denounce the intrinsic wickedness of the Church, if they knew that it was wicked; these may be classed as Christian. But a good Catholic is necessarily an enemy of Christianity.

3. THE PERIOD OF METAMORPHOSIS (380 A.D. TO 1302 A.D.—922 YEARS)

The decree of Theodosius which ended the parallel period also opened the period of metamorphosis. His decree was: "We command all who read this law to embrace the name of Catholic Christians, deciding that all other idiots and madmen should bear the infa-

my attached to their heretical opinions, and as they
will first meet with the penalty of divine vengeance,
so they will afterwards receive that condemnation at
our hands which the heavenly judge has empowered
us to administer." By winking at this the early
Church surrendered to paganism. The royal edict
should have been denounced in the same manner that
the early Church refused to worship the Emperor.
"Gratian followed in the West the example which
Theodosius had set in the East. He was the first
to decline the dignity of Pontifex Maximus."

After the virus of the death penalty for heresy
filled the veins of the organism, it was only a question of time when the disease would break out in
"wounds and bruises and putrefying sores." Only
five brief years elapsed until the telltale infallible
sympton of paganism appeared. "The execution of
religious dissenters was begun in 385 with the death
of the Priscillianists at Treves. Fathers of the
ancient Church exhausted the dictionary for severe
words to stigmatize heretics. Athanasius called
them dogs, wolves, and worse. The Donatists were
likened to scabby sheep and to the locusts of Joel
hidden in the dust. Heresy was a cancer to be cut out
by the extermination of the heretic."[1]

The fact that the application of the Theodosian
law against heretics caused a profound sensation
throughout the Catholic world shows that such measures were not regarded by the Christians at that time
as being in harmony with the methods of the early
Church.

---

[1]"The Church," by John Huss, translated by David S.
Schaff.

In tracing the genealogy of the Roman Catholic Church we shall ignore the idea of "apostolic succession." When we reach Theodosius in our investigation we shall follow the Roman emperors and not the popes.

We are warranted in this by the fact that Damasus I. (pope 366–384; afterwards made a saint) "lived to welcome the famous edict of Theodosius I., *'De fide Catholica'* (February 27, 380), which proclaimed as the religion of the Roman State that doctrine which Saint Peter had preached to the Romans and of which Damasus was supreme head."[2]

It was Damasus who brought Romanism into its own. Neither Constantine nor the popes of his epoch were so daring as to attempt murder in the name of Christ. There was plenty of heathenism before Theodosius and Damasus, but it was groping its way into a new world. The primacy of the apostolic See was "variously favored in the time of Damasus by *imperial acts and edicts*," and "was strenuously maintained by this pope." Besides, the fraudulent "Decretals" upon which the blasphemous papal supremacy was afterwards built are placed by the Catholic Encyclopedia in the age of Damasus. "This development of the papal office, especially in the West, brought with it a great increase of external grandeur." Damasus "provided for the proper housing of the archives of the Roman Church." He also built a marble monument on the Appian Way in honor of the temporary transfer to that place (258) of Saint Peter and Saint Paul and he built in the Vatican a baptistery in honor of Saint Peter.

[2]Catholic Encyclopedia, Vol. IV., page 613.

Theodosius, in the early part of 380, was baptized by the Catholic Bishop of Thessalonica. "One of his last acts was a despairing appeal to the sword, which offers again the dramatic situation of a field of battle on which the religion of Europe seemed to depend." Theodosius definitely abandoned the title of Pontifex Maximus; from this time on the Roman popes assumed that title, or whatever the title implied, as their exclusive property. We see then that Theodosius was a Roman Catholic, that he officially inaugurated the bloody and diabolical *régime* of murdering heretics in the name of Christianity, that the then reigning pope (Damasus) fully accepted the *régime*, that Theodosius remained both bloody and Romish up to his death, and that the old superstitious, priestly, idolatrous State religion of ancient Rome quietly changed its garb and took hold of the empire in the name of the Nazarene.

Before Theodosius's time the heads of the Roman Church were the Roman emperors; after Theodosius, they were the Roman popes. The emperors were primarily heads of the State, but they had full control of all that was vital in religion; the popes were also primarily at the head of the State and had full control over everything that was vital in religion.

Before Theodosius's time and for some time afterwards the popes were often quite decent; all of them were canonized and perhaps a number of them deserved some such recognition. Rome canonized fifty-four popes during four hundred and eighty-five years (41–526) at the beginning of her history. But for the next seven hundred and sixty-four years

(530–1294) the saint-makers found only twenty-three popes fit material for such dignity.

By the year 1294 the papal contention for supremacy over civil government was virtually realized. It was a rickety throne on which the pontiffs sat, but they have till this good day done their worst to balance themselves at the height of their pseudo imperialism. It is very significant that during the six hundred and twenty-three years from the date on which Boniface VIII. declared that he was Cæsar and emperor (1300) down to the present time only one (Pius V., 1566–1572) of the seventy-one popes who have graced and disgraced the chair has attained sainthood, and before his election he was the chief inquisitor. Can it be that Rome could afford to recognize as eminently holy only one of her threescore and ten chief bishops during these important six centuries, and this one because he was a cruel and unscrupulous fanatic? It is also significant that the last papal saint before the inquisitorial Pius was too religious to remain even one year in his pontifical seat. Moreover, his successor, Boniface—the one who said that he was Cæsar and who issued the infamous bull *Unam Sanctam*—imprisoned the devout Celestine V. and kept him there until the pious monk wasted away and died.

The Cæsarean Succession of the Roman Church

By neglecting the emperors of little significance, we may trace the Roman Catholic Church from the time of Christ down to 380 A.D. as follows; Augustus Cæsar (31 B.C. to 14 A.D.), Tiberius, Caligula, Claudius, Nero, Vespasian, Titus, Domitian, Nerva,

Trajan, Hadrian, Antoninus Pius, Marcus Aurelius, Commodus, Claudius, Aurelian, Diocletian, Constantine, Julian the Apostate, Valentinian, Theodosius—total number, twenty-one.

By adding the two hundred and twenty-nine popes who have reigned since Theodosius to the twenty-one emperors in this list we have two hundred and fifty Roman Pontiffs from the time the Church began— that is, 27 B.C. This will do for practical purposes; we may ignore the twoscore other emperors whom we have not included in the above list.

It is only important that we keep the record clear. The bishops at Rome were not universal during the four first centuries; moreover, they did not officially incriminate themselves in bloody decrees against good people.

Following the pagan decree of Theodosius, all the atrocities which were directed against the natural right of men to think were only the development of the heathen germ.

Before this time murder in the name of religion, ritualism, image worship, holy water, the merit of external works, fanatical martyrdom, indiscriminate almsgiving, the profligacy of the higher clergy, and the assumption of temporal power over the conscience were slowly dominating the Church. This is the heathen order; first ceremonialism, then the subordination of morals and personal rights, then the murder of those who oppose the supremacy of hocus-pocus.

Such an unreasonable and wicked scheme of religion and morals could not conquer at a single bound; the best sentiments and thoughts of those

who had the New Testament in their hands could not
be suppressed at once. Leo. I. (440–461) has been
called the founder of the medieval policy; but his
system needed a little more development, for he
recognized the superiority of the emperor; it was
logical that the emperor should be controlled rather
than supplicated. This goal was speedily reached in
theory, but the masses of Europe had to be degraded.
The pope took over the title of Pontifex Maximus
when the Western Empire fell, but the scheme was
not yet compact; he had to act through the emperor.
His organization wanted only one thing more, and
that was for the pope to grasp the imperial scepter.
This tremendous task was accomplished between
380 and 1302. But God Almighty would not allow
a complete triumph of wrong, although he did wait
long before the time came for his Spirit to assert his
supremacy in the individual heart. "The history of
Europe from the fifth century onward to the fifteenth
is largely the history of the failure of this great idea of
a divine world government to realize itself in practice."[3]

Meanwhile sects were not wanting who rebelled
against this unholy alliance of Christianity with
paganism.

The Donatists first rose up in favor of the doctrine
that a priest living in mortal sin could not validly
perform the sacraments; as a result they were formally condemned as heretical. This sect continued from
the third to the seventh century. Thus the Romish
Church early began its vicious habit of cursing and
swearing at good people. As in later centuries their

---

[3]"Outline of History," Wells, Vol. I., page 605.

9

blasphemy failed; the truth of God could not be entirely crushed.

After this came the Paulicians, beginning their career in the seventh century and finally merging in the Albigenses. These were above reproach in their morals; they objected to images, the sacraments, the (magical) symbol of the cross, and the worship of Mary.

The Albigenses developed rapidly in the ninth century and, after filling an essential place in their protest against the iniquities of Romanism, they were all but exterminated in 1229.

The Waldenses began their important work in 1170 and preserved until the Reformation the vital principles which had been conserved and defended at the price of blood, by the Donatists, the Paulicians, the Albigenses, and other heretical sects whose righteous souls were vexed every day with the ungodly conversation and conduct of the higher clergy.

However widely those sects may have differed among themselves or from each other during the early and the medieval centuries, one basic truth ran through all their beliefs—*the need of moral character on the part of the priest*. The one thing for which the Catholic Church had always contended was that magic and not morals was indispensable to the priest.

The medieval period was not one of gradual absorption of heathen ideas by the Catholic Church; that Church began its so-called Christian career just as it ended the second epoch of its existence. Now that Christianity had been outlawed, it must be humiliated into submissiveness. All the seven sacraments of the Romish Church were and are a criminal

of Mohammedanism were resisted, and the flame of devotion was kept burning, though more or less darkened by superstition. But this does not prove that the Church was Christian. Pagan Rome did all such things, except preserve the Holy Scriptures, and the heretics could have taken care of the Bible as did the despised Jews in Babylon.

While all this was going on the pagan spirit rapidly recovered its original vigor and prestige. It had only been apparently defeated. The objective now was to merge the head of the State and the head of the Church into one person, just as it was when Augustus Cæsar was supreme in both civil and religious realms. By declaring the Christian religion to be the exclusive religion of the Empire, Theodosius opened the way for the infant Church to degrade herself and become a heathen religion. *By accepting the Emperor's decree the Church became a purely pagan religion.* The germ continued to grow until Pope Gregory III. (731–741) claimed temporal power, excommunicated the Eastern Emperor, and asked Charles Martel to hasten to the succor of the "Holy Church." *The donation of the States of the Church to Pope Stephen II. by Pepin (775) was a decisive victory of paganism over the languishing Christian elements which persisted.* Heathenism publicly and formally asserted herself when Pope Leo III. crowned Charles the Great on Christmas (800). That emperor was then called the sixty-eighth successor of the first Roman Cæsar. In the spirit of Mohammed his motto was, "Christianity or death." Nicholas I. (858–867) asserted the supremacy of the pope over civil government. "All the rulers of the earth," it was declared, "are bound to obey the bishop and to bow the neck before him." Hildebrand (Gregory VII., 1073–1085) fully carried out the program which Nicholas only partially achieved. Innocent III. (1098–1216) continued the policy and the theory of Hildebrand. He it was who would fain have throttled the famous movement in England, which preserved in that country and bequeathed to the United States the liberty enjoyed by these two countries to-day. In his bull, *Esti Charissimus*, Innocent curses the Magna Charta in these words:

We . . . do hereby, in the name of the Holy Trinity, and by the authority of the Apostles Paul and Peter and our own, altogether condemn and reprobate the said compact or charter; and do prohibit the king, under pain of anathema, to observe and keep the same; and the barons of England and their accomplices to insist upon or stand by it; and we hereby render null and void the said charter, together with all obligations and securities entered into in pursuance or execution thereof, so that it be void and of none effect for all time to come.[4]

Boniface VIII., at the jubilee of 1300, "seated on the throne of Constantine, girded with the imperial sword, wearing a crown, and waving a scepter," shouted; "I am Cæsar, I am Emperor." This closed the period during which the medieval Church deliberately and finally rejected everything distinctively Christian.

Paganism has always regarded power as primary and morals as secondary. To please the gods by means of hocus-pocus never had any permanent relation to right living. Augustus Cæsar, Theodosius,

---

[4] *"Bullarium Magnum Romanum,"* Tomus III., pages 298-300. See *The Protestant*, March, 1921.

Gregory III., Stephen II., Leo III., Nicholas I., Gregory VII., Innocent III., and Boniface VIII. held the same idea, that civil government had the right to control the human conscience according to ritual. This brought them all into conflict with the higher ideals of those who placed character above the pleasure of the gods or of the agents of the gods.

The task of the Church during the Middle Ages was similar to that of the muddauber wasp, which collects spiders, preserves them by a thrust of its sting through the nerve ganglia, and saves them as food for her larvæ. Roman paganism made a new acquisition when she conquered Christianity. It was now necessary to stigmatize everything in Christianity which was incompatible with paganism. Love of enemies, the "priesthood of believers," the need of righteousness in the ministry, respect for civil law, the use of spiritual means for spiritual conquest, purity and humility as superior to sacraments, were some of the things taught by Jesus Christ.

Jesus made ethics an outstanding characteristic of his system. Heathenism required first of all conformity to established religion. It cannot be proven that subjection to the pope of Rome fosters morals; it can be demonstrated that it did make murderers and thieves out of thousands of men and women who obeyed the pontiff in the extermination of heretics and the confiscation of their property. This rampant ferocity was not gradually introduced; it was implicit the very day that Theodosius proclaimed that Christianity was the exclusive religion of the Empire. There was not a single day of interregnum between the close of the pagan period and the beginning of what is usually called the medieval Christian era. The continuity of the religion of pagan Rome is an astonishing phenomenon. In all its essentials it is now precisely what it was before Christ, also during the time it was a rival of Christianity, and during the whole medieval period and until now.

By the close of the career of Gregory the Great (604) "the papacy of the Middle Ages had been born."

The hierarchy of officers had been practically completed. There was a marked evolution in rites and ceremonies. . . . The Mass gradually became the powerful mysterious center of all worship, while public worship became imposing, dramatic, theatrical. Festivals were multiplied almost without number. The worship of martyrs and saints became so widespread and popular that a "calendar of saints" was formed. Pilgrimages grew to be very numerous and the use of relics developed such a craze that the fathers, councils, popes, and at last the Emperor sought to check it. Religious pageants were multiplied and the use of images and pictures of saints was encouraged in the churches. The Virgin Mary was exalted to the eminence of divinity. . . . Saint Chrysostom sharply rebuked the bishops who "had fallen to the condition of land stewards, hucksters, brokers, publicans, and pay clerks." [5]

Like the wasp referred to above, the original pagan religion of Rome had stung the moral nerve of Christianity so that all the distinctive doctrines of Christianity could be demolished at leisure. When it was no longer necessary for the Catholic Church even to pretend to possess the Christian virtues, she became frenzied over all forms of opposition. Yet this did not extirpate the faith nor the faithful. Lindsay

---

[5] "The Rise of the Medieval Church," pages 193, 194.

shows clearly that there were great numbers of good, quiet, devout, humble, God-fearing people who did not absorb the impiety of the official religion.[6]

The very persistence of these Christians, whether within the Church or whether members of non-conformist bodies, only angered the representatives of Romanism. There was now no more hope of converting this Church, which was in 1302 at least nineteen hundred years old in all the essentials of its constitution and more than nine hundred years old in its new rôle. And yet a few more touches of the brush were required before a perfect picture of paganism could be presented to the world.

4. THE FRANTIC PERIOD (1302–1870—568 YEARS)

The bull, *Unam Sanctam*, of Boniface VIII., is an *ex-cathedra* document. All Catholics, everywhere and in all ages, are bound to believe and profess it. This bull ushers in the epoch in which Christianity is officially repudiated. The nobler members of the Church now had to find some way to live secret Christian lives in spite of the blatant paganism of their own religious system, or else protest and suffer the consequences.

For five hundred and seventy years the fight had been between the laity and the hierarchy, between the moral and thoughtful on the one hand and the devotees of magic and ambition on the other. Since the hierarchy had permanently turned traitor to Jesus Christ, either the laity, the moral and reasoning element, must get control and reform the clergy,

---

[6]Consult "History of the Reformation," Vol. I., pages 125, 126, 139, 140, 146, 152, 153.

both as to their teaching and conduct, or the priest-hood must maintain the doctrine of a priestly caste with magical powers with which to enslave the masses.

In 1517 Martin Luther put forth his ninety-five theses at Wittenberg and the way was opened for thoughtful, conscientious Christians to leave the pagan Catholic Church.

From 1545 to 1563 the Council of Trent sat inter-mittently and deliberated as to how that Church might win back the Protestants without reforming the lives of the clergy or surrendering their right to kill those who opposed the immoralities and idolatries of Romanism.

Students of history will note that from the time (1302) when the tiger spirit took complete possession of the Church, until the Vatican Council (568 years), when the Romish evolution was complete, it could not be said any more that Catholicism tamed savage tribes, or led in the paths of progress, or stood as a beacon light to those in darkness. Her own son, Christopher Columbus, was permitted to discover a new country, but "Mother Church" deserves no credit for it. A Galileo was allowed to remain in the ark of salvation—after asserting that the earth re-volved on its axis and around the sun—provided that he would stultify his conscience and thus demonstrate that he was still a good Catholic. The deplorable condition of all Latin America, the scene of Rome's greatest missionary activities during the frantic pe-riod, proves conclusively that she was anti-Christian in all that propaganda.

During this era, after the pope had asserted his

lordship over all the earth in such terms as to bind all Catholics forever, down to the time when the States of the Church were lost, the rage of hell was turned loose on the world. It was during this time that Jerome of Prague and John Huss were burned for the crime of being Christians and preaching Christian doctrine.

Huss declared: "The Roman Church is not the Catholic apostolic Church." He held that the pope was not the bond of Christian unity, the Church was not inerrant; that the pope might be a heretic and that previous to the fifteenth century there had been both wicked men and heretics in the papal chair; that the pope was not the head of the Church, for that would mean that the Church was without a head, as in the interims between the death of one pontiff and the election of his successor; that to rebel against an erring pope was to obey God; and that the power of the keys, or the authority to remit sins or retain them, was simply a declaratory power such as the priest in the old dispensation exercised in pronouncing the leper clean and as the disciples exercised in loosing Lazarus. The priest did not make the leper clean, nor did the disciples release Lazarus from the bonds of death. He held that the pope did not possess the power of the keys in the way generally supposed, as a thing of his own; if he did, then he might empty purgatory itself, and, if he neglected to do so, he would be guilty of ill-will or indifference. With Wycliffe, and upon the basis of the Lord's Prayer, Huss held that in a real sense every Christian has the right to absolve. He taught that the Scriptures are the supreme rule of faith and conduct.

He also took solemn issue with the theory and the
practice of the medieval Church as regards the death
penalty for heresy. All this implied the exercise of
private judgment.[7]

These doctrines were the doctrines of the early
Church and of the Protestants to-day. The great
scholar, Jerome of Prague (1365–1416), disciple and
defender of Huss, held the same views and, like Huss,
was burned at the stake.[8]

Ancient pagan Rome persecuted, it is true, but
mildly as compared with the atrocities committed by
the Roman Catholic Church during the medieval era.
The history of Europe for five hundred years, from
the twelfth to the seventeenth century, "was the
history of the efforts of the Church, with open force
or secret conspiracy, with all the energy, base or
noble, which passion or passionate enthusiasm could
inspire, to crush and annihilate its foes. No means
came amiss to it, sword or stake, torture chamber or
assassin's dagger. The effects of the Church's
working were seen in the ruined nations and smoking
cities, in human beings tearing one another to pieces
like raging maniacs, and the honor of the Creator of
the world befouled by the hideous crimes committed
in his name." The height of Catholic ferocity was
reached several centuries before Boniface made his
blasphemous declaration; but it is charitably con-
ceded that Christianity was slightly recognized in
some inscrutable way until the bull, *Unam Sanctam*,

---

[7]See "The Church," by John Huss, translated, with notes
and introduction, by David S. Schaff.
[8]Encyclopedia Britannica, Vol. XII. (Ninth Edition.)

settled for all time the fact that Romanism was completely pagan.

5. THE VENOMOUS PERIOD (FROM 1870 FORWARD)

After the leaders of Romanism had virtually declared themselves to be wholly pagan and anti-Christian, as if to make assurance doubly sure, the bishops met in solemn conclave in the Vatican at Rome in 1870 and proclaimed the complete triumph of heathenism in what is known as the doctrine of the Infallibility of the Pope. The decree is to the effect that the pope, when he speaks *ex-cathedra*—that is, as pope—to the whole Christian (Catholic) world, on matters pertaining to faith and morals, giving a definition as to what must be believed, cannot err, and that his decrees cannot be reformed, also that his authority is not from the consent of the Church.

This decree undermines morals in three ways: (1) It places ceremonies on a still higher pedestal than they were before, for the pope is henceforth completely in charge of Romish rites; (2) it solidifies his supremacy over civil government, which is unscriptural and destructive of morals and religion; (3) it makes the immoral casuistry of Romanism unchangeable.

Practically the popes do not concern themselves with matters of everyday morals, but turn those questions over to the theologians. Modern popes have not only ceded the whole territory of morals to Liguori, but they have deliberately set their seal to his teachings. When he was canonized it had to be done by the pope, and the pope could not do it until his writings were pronounced by the duly constituted assault on the citadel of moral character. The sacrament of order is a direct attack on the right of the individual to understand his Bible, and it is an unscrupulous assault on devout scholarship among non-Catholics. Penance and absolution with the secrecy and the dangers of the confessional are a blasphemous attempt to enter the secret chambers of the human soul where God alone has the right or the power to dwell. Transubstantiation would undermine the right of human beings to accept the testimony of their five senses; this tears down the foundations of science. The doctrine that the sacraments carry grace in and of themselves reduces morality to a subordinate place and makes it a mechanical affair.

The effects of all these fundamental errors are seen in the family, where the priest insinuates himself between husband and wife, between parents and children; also in the civil government, where the pope asserts superiority to trained and conscientious statesmen; in the intellectual world, where dogma asserts its supremacy over reason and over the facts of science.

While the principles inculcated by Jesus Christ were being eliminated from the heathen organism, and before the process was complete, it was impossible even for official Romanism wholly to neutralize their beneficent effects. It was during this anomalous era that the Church was able to tame savage tribes, encourage letters, and give asylum to the unfortunate and oppressed. It arbitrated great questions of government and preserved the Holy Scriptures. Unity was fostered among the faithful, the onslaughts theologians to be free from error; that was done. In addition to that he is called the "prince of moral theologians," and a "doctor" of the Church. He was "decreed the rank of 'Venerable,' being so named by Pius VI. in 1796;" his writings were declared to be free from error by a decree of Pius VII., in 1804; Pope Gregory XVI. in 1849 declared him a saint and reaffirmed his perfect orthodoxy. Pope Pius IX. not only places Liguori alongside Thomas Aquinas and others, but he makes him "the sole authoritative interpreter of all moral theologians earlier than himself.[9]

We have recounted briefly the history of Romanism in order to demonstrate that the Catholic Church which we are studying, the Catholic Church with which we constantly deal on the mission field, the Catholic Church which lives and thrives in the twentieth century and especially in Protestant countries, is the religion which began before the birth of Christ and which has continued steadily through the centuries.

Papal Paganism put an end to the Christian Church, as a unified body scattered over the Empire, in the year 380 A.D. The heathen principles which were intrinsic in the Roman Catholic Church at that time required fourteen hundred and ninety years to develop. At the Vatican Council in 1870 the last dogma worthy of consideration (papal infallibility) was deliberately pronounced. Nothing is left to the hierarchy now but to bite and poison their enemies. Romish theologians take great pains to show that all

---

[9]See Encyclopedia Britannica, Ninth Edition, article on *Liguori*.

the paganism of modern Catholicism began before
the Medieval Period. That is correct. The Christian Church from 380 to the present time has been
diffused throughout Europe, America, and other
parts of the world; manifested under a variety of
names; but always with the same marks. On the
other hand, the supremacy of morals, the preëminence
of the grace of God, the "priesthood of believers," a
spiritual religion without union of Church and State,
are among the infallible evidences of the simple
religion given us by the Nazarene.

When we examine all the cardinal pagan elements
which have been preserved and developed by Romanism; when we analyze these in their nature and
their effects on the individual; when we look abroad
among the nations and discover how these elements
have wrought havoc everywhere, we are amazed at
the vastness of the scheme. It is the marvel of the
ages how human ambition could have employed so
successfully the seemingly innate superstitions of
men on so tremendous a scale and for so long a time.
But we must remember that all this is not confined
to papalism; more than four-fifths of the human race
are being exploited in the same way, with this difference, that the religion of Italy is the most thoroughly perverse and aggressive of them all.

PART II

THE TRUCELESS WAR BETWEEN ROMAN-ISM AND CHRISTIANITY

When Christianity began her glorious career, the world had exhausted its strength in trying to debase itself, and to sink low enough to embrace paganism; and yet not so low as not to try to exist in the shape of nations. The experiment had been repeated, times we know not how many. Egypt, Babylonia, Persia, polished Greece, iron-footed Rome, mystical Hinduism, had all tried it. They spent, each, mind enough to regenerate a nation, in trying to build up a system of corrupt paganism; and when that system was built up—let the shape and form be what it might—the nation had exhausted its energies, and it sunk and fell under the effects of misapplied and perverted mind. . . . Another striking instance of the perversion of mind, and the abuse of the human intellect and heart, is the system of the Roman Church. No one created mind, apparently, could ever have invented a scheme of delusion, of degradation of the soul, the intellect, the whole man, so perfect and complete as this. What minds must have been employed in shutting out the light of heaven, and in burying the manna which fell in showers so extended! What a system!—And when the Reformation held up all these abominations to light, what a masterpiece was the last plan to stifle the reason forever—the Inquisition! . . . The ingenuity of hell seemed tasked to invent methods by which the human mind might be shut up in Egyptian darkness; and never was a Catholic community known to be other than degraded, ignorant, superstitious, and sunken. . . . But what a mass of mind has been, and still is, employed in upholding this sytem! And what a loss to the world has it produced, in quenching, in everlasting darkness, the uncounted millions of glorious minds which have been destroyed by it.[10]

[10] Todd's "Student's Manual," pages 356–358.

(144)

CHAPTER V

THE THOROUGHLY ANTI-CHRISTIAN CHARACTER OF ROMANISM

OF all the marvelous feats ever performed by the Romish hierarchy or by any other group of unscrupulous men, the greatest is that by which the modern theologians of America have been drilled to say to their constituency that Romanism and Christianity have a common origin, a common purpose, a common groundwork of faith. Catholic theologians are careful to maintain the genuine Romish thesis that the two systems are radically different from each other. But the advanced theological thinkers of this country seem to be capable of practicing a miraculous simplicity in slipping the noose over their own heads and following their artful leaders wherever they are told to go. The marvel is that while these designing priests lead their Protestant disciples in one direction they themselves go in the opposite direction.

It is refreshing to those of us who wish to trace effects back to their real causes to find that at least some of the greatest scholars in the world are able to discern.

Adolph Harnack has done some independent thinking. His estimate of Romanism in its nature and origin is well worth pondering. In his description of Greek Catholicism he smashes any sort of pretensions to apostolicity or Christianity as follows:

What are the characteristics of this Church? . . . No one can look at this Church from the outside, with its forms of

10   (145)

worship, its solemn ritual, the number of its ceremonies, its relics, pictures, priests, monks, and the philosophy of its mysteries, and then compare it on the one hand with the Hellenic cults in the age of Neoplatonism, without arriving at the conclusion that it belongs not to the former but to the latter. It takes the form, not of a Christian product in Greek dress, but of a Greek product in Christian dress. It would have done battle with the Christians of the first century just as it did battle with the worship of Magna Mater and Zeus Soter. There are innumerable features of this Church which are counted as sacred as the gospel, and toward which not even a tendency existed in primitive Christianity. Of the whole performance of the chief religious service—nay, even of many of the dogmas—the same thing may, in the last resort, be said: if certain words, like "Christ," etc., are omitted, there is nothing left to recall the original element. In its external form as a whole this Church is nothing more than a continuation of the history of Greek religion under the alien influence of Christianity, parallel to the many other alien influences which have affected it. . . . There is no sadder spectacle than this transformation of the Christian religion from a worship of God in spirit and in truth into a worship of God in signs, formulas, and idols. . . . Where . . . can we find in Jesus's message even a trace of any injunction that a man is to submit to solemn ceremonies as though they were mysterious ministrations, to be punctilious in observing a ritual, to put up pictures, and to mumble maxims and formulas in a prescribed fashion? It was to destroy this sort of religion that Jesus Christ suffered himself to be nailed to the cross, and now we find it reëstablished under his name and authority! . . . What modifications did the gospel undergo in this Church and how did it hold its own? Well, in the first place, I do not expect to be contradicted if I answer that this official ecclesiasticism, with its priests and its cult, with all its vessels, saints, vestments, pictures, and amulets, with its ordinances of fasting and its festivals, has absolutely nothing to do with the religion of Christ. It is the religion of the ancient world tacked on to certain conceptions in the gospel; or, rather, it is the ancient religion with the gospel absorbed into it.[1]

---

[1] "What Is Christianity?" pages 236, 237, 255, 258.

Turning to Roman Catholicism, the learned author observes:

The element which the Roman Church shares with the Greeks must, then, be of significant and critical importance, when it is sufficient to make union possible on the condition that the papal supremacy is recognized. As a matter of fact, the main points characteristic of Greek Catholicism are all to be found in Roman as well, and are, on occasion, just as energetically maintained here as they are there. Traditionalism, orthodoxy, and ritualism play just the same part here as they do there. . . . In Rome the episcopal throne was occupied in the fifth century by men who understood the signs of the times and utilized them to the full. *The Roman Church in this way privily pushed itself into the place of the Roman World-Empire, of which it is the actual continuation;* the empire has not perished, but has only undergone a transformation. If we assert, and mean the assertion to hold good even of the present time, that the Roman Church is the old Roman Empire consecrated by the gospel, that is no mere clever remark, but the recognition of the matter historically, and the most appropriate and fruitful way of describing the character of this Church. It still governs the nations; its popes rule like Trajan and Marcus Aurelius; Peter and Paul have taken the place of Romulus and Remus; the bishops and archbishops, of the proconsuls; the troops of priests and monks correspond to the legions; the Jesuits, to the imperial bodyguard. The continued influence of the old Empire and its institutions may be traced in detail, down to individual legal ordinances—nay, even in the very clothes. That is no Church like the evangelical communities, or the national Churches of the East; *it is a political creation, and as imposing as a World-Empire, because the continuation of the Roman Empire.* The pope, who calls himself "King" and "Pontifex Maximus," is Cæsar's successor. The Church, which as early as the third and fourth century was entirely filled with the Roman spirit, has reëstablished in itself the Roman Empire. Nor have patriotic Catholics in Rome and Italy in every century from the seventh and eighth onward understood the matter otherwise. . . . What modifications has the gospel here undergone, and how much of it is left?

Well—this is not a matter that needs many words—the whole
outward and visible institution of a Church claiming divine
dignity has no foundation whatever in the gospel. *It is a
case, not of distortion, but of total perversion.* Religion has here
strayed away in a direction that is not its own. As Eastern
Catholicism may in many respects be more appropriately
regarded as part of the history of Greek religion than of the
history of the gospel, so Roman Catholicism must be regarded
as part of the history of the Roman World-Empire. To contend, as it does, that Christ founded a kingdom; that this
kingdom is the Roman Church; that he equipped it with a
sword—nay, with two swords, a spiritual and a temporal—is
to secularize the gospel; nor can this contention be sustained
by appealing to the idea that Christ's spirit ought certainly to
bear rule amongst mankind. The gospel says, "Christ's
kingdom is not of this world," but the Church has set up an
earthly kingdom; Christ demands that his ministers shall not
rule but serve, but here the priests govern the world; Christ
leads his disciples away from political and ceremonious religion and places every man face to face with God—God and
the soul, the soul and its God; but here, on the contrary, man
is bound to an earthly institution with chains that cannot be
broken, and he must obey; it is only when he obeys that he
approaches God.[2]

Auguste Sabatier has the same opinion as that of
Harnack:

Transplanted from the dry and poor soil of Judaism to
the rich and powerful humus of the Græco-Roman civilization, the Christian plant should have grown and transformed
itself. Just as apostolic Messianism was Jewish, so was Catholicism pagan, from the same causes and following the same
law. More Greek in the East, more Roman in the West, it
yet bears everywhere and always the marks of its origin. If
you will study the Catholic Church successively in all its
phases, you will find in every one of them this indelible mark.
Take, for example, the dogmas of the councils and the the-

[2]"What Is Christianity?" pages 266, 267, 269–271, 280, 281.

ology of the fathers; who does not see at once their true character? Who does not see that the warp and woof are Greek; in form, in color, and in every thread that enters into it? Whence came those terms and ideas which, from their beginning on, the theologians fling as darts and which were unknown in the Hebrew; abstract terms of substance and hypostasis, of nature and person, of essence and accidents, of matter and form? Whence came the science of the fathers of the Church, their exegesis, their history, their logic, their psychology, and that sublime metaphysics which transformed so completely the heaven of the prophets into the Platonic heaven? All this comes from Athens, from Ephesus, from Samos, from Miletus, passing first through Alexandria and Rome. Justin, Athenagoras, Clement, and Basil—even more than Arius, Jerome, and Augustine—were fed from their infancy on Greek and Latin literature. They read Plato, Heraclitus, Zeno, Philo, also Cicero, Posidonius, and Seneca, as much as, perhaps more than, the Old Testament. Why should it seem strange that their theology should little by little pass over to Neoplatonism until that philosophy should become for Augustine the real introduction to the gospel, and that in the Middle Ages the names of Plato and Aristotle should have no less authority than those of Isaiah, Saint Paul, and Saint Peter?

Let us pass to the constitution of the Church. What is it but an exact reproduction of the constitution of the Roman Empire? The parish is modeled after the city, the diocese after the province, the metropolitan regions after the large prefectures. At the apex of the pyramid is the pope, whose ideal dream is nothing less in the religious realm than the universal and absolute monarchy whose image was first envisaged by the Cæsars. True it is that at its origin and as long as the persecutions continued there was much friction between Jewish or Christian customs and those of Greek and Roman society. But with time the difference is singularly diminished. If the Church is to conquer the world, the world will get revenge on the Church, so that when, with Constantine, the union and fusion are almost complete, we would hesitate to say whether the ancient world has become Christian or whether Christianity has become paganized. What is monkish

asceticism, imposing celibacy on the clergy and exalting
virginity, multiplying pious works to increase the merits of
devotion, replacing those duties which nature and society
create with fictitious and worthless duties? Is it not simply the
result of a dualism and the imitation of an ideal which,
originating in the Orient, would seduce the feverish imagina-
tions of a dying world? Did monks and anchorites and the
theologies of impotent celibates save Egypt or Syria or Byzan-
tium?

What of the cult, the worship, and everything properly
called religion during all this time? Between heaven and
earth there are seen to reappear all the ancient hierarchy of
gods, semigods, heroes, nymphs, or goddesses, replaced by the
Virgin mother, angels, devils, and saints. Every village,
every parish, every fountain has its patron saint, its titular
guard, to whom the populace appeal with more familiarity
than to God in order to obtain the temporal blessings and
graces for each day. The saints have their special tasks, as
did the little gods of former times. One cures the fever, while
another heals diseases of the skin. This one protects travelers,
while that one guards the harvest or heals the flocks; a third
is omnipotent in finding lost objects or in giving to heirs their
houses which are likely to be lost to them. With this my-
thology is reborn all the old superstitions, including plain
fetishism. Pilgrimages, prayers, and litanies, the veneration
of images and of relics, the sign of the cross, signs and sacraments are all conceived and performed according to the
ancient mysteries. All of this was done in a sort of uncon-
scious way, by a kind of slow process, and frequently as the
effect of a zeal which was reputed as Christian. The leaders
of the Church recommended to the missionaries that they
should not destroy the temples of the false gods, but that they
should consecrate them to the true, replacing their images with
the images of the saints, and the rites of the ancient cult with
similar ceremonies. Thus were changed the names and the
formalities, but not the heart of the religion. In Rome under
the basilica of Saint Peter a proud statue of the Prince of the
Apostles is erected. There in other days stood a statue of
Jupiter. The foot is worn by the kisses of the faithful. Before the days of Christianity they kissed the feet of the god of

gods; since the dawn of the Christian era, they kiss the foot of Peter. Is the worship therefore different, even in that of a superior devotion?[3]

John Wesley took the position that the papacy was pre-Christian in its origin and always pagan in its nature. In his "Notes on the New Testament" he states the case in several comments. On 2 Thessalonians ii. 2–4, "Let no man deceive you by any means, for that day shall not come, unless the falling away come first, and the man of sin be revealed, the son of perdition; who opposeth and exalteth himself above all that is called God, or that is worshiped, so that he sitteth in the temple of God as God, declaring himself that he is God." Comment:

> *The man of sin, the son of perdition*—Eminently so called, is not yet come. However, in many respects, the pope has an indisputable claim to those titles. He is, in an emphatical sense, the man of sin, as he increases all manner of sin above measure. And he is too properly styled, the son of perdition, as he has caused the death of numberless multitudes, both of his opposers and followers, destroyed innumerable souls, and will himself perish everlastingly. He it is that opposeth himself to the emperor, once his rightful sovereign; and that *exalteth himself above all that is called God, or that is worshiped* —Commanding angels, and putting kings under his feet, both of whom are called gods in Scripture; claiming the highest power, the highest honor; suffering himself not once only to be styled God or vice-god. Indeed no less is implied in his ordinary title, Most holy Lord, or Most holy Father. *So that he sitteth*—Enthroned, in the temple of God—mentioned Revelation xi. 1, *declaring himself that he is God*—Claiming the prerogatives which belong to God alone.

It is remarkable how Mr. Wesley saw the papal

---

[3]"Essay on a Philosophy of Religion," by Auguste Sabatier, pages 216–218. Translated from the Spanish version of Eduardo Ovejéro y Maury, by J. A. P.

tendency to a still greater blasphemy and iniquity
than had been realized in his time or during the Middle Ages. Says he:

The whole succession of popes from Gregory VII. are un-
doubtedly antichrist. Yet this hinders not, but that the last
pope in this succession will be more eminently the antichrist,
the man of sin; adding to that of his predecessors a peculiar
degree of wickedness from the bottomless pit. This individual
person, as a pope, is the seventh head of the beast; as the man
of sin, he is the eighth, or the beast himself.[4]

Seventy-nine years after Mr. Wesley's death the
pope was pronounced infallible; from that time till
now, and to the end of the papacy, the pope is in a
special way "the beast himself."

As to the origin of the Romish religion (Rev. xiii.
2), where it is stated that the beast receives his power
from the dragon, Mr. Wesley explains:

The three first beasts in Daniel are like a leopard, a bear,
and a lion. In all parts, except his feet and mouth, this beast
was like a leopard, or female panther; which is fierce as a lion,
or bear, and is also swift and subtle. Such is the papacy,
which has, partly by subtlety, partly by force, gained power
over so many nations. The extremely various usages, manners, and ways of the pope, may likewise be compared to the
spots of the leopard. *And his feet were as the feet of a bear*—
Which are very strong, and armed with sharp claws. And as
clumsy as they seem, he can therewith walk, stand upright,
climb, or seize anything. So does this beast seize and take
for his prey whatever comes within the reach of his claws;
and his mouth was as the mouth of a lion—To roar, and to de-
vour. *And the dragon*—Whose vassal and vicegerent he is,
gave him his power—His own strength and innumerable forces,
and his throne—So that he might command whatever he
would, having great, absolute authority. The dragon had his
throne in heathen Rome, so long as idolatry and persecution

<hr>

[4]On Revelation xvii. 11.

reigned there. And after he was disturbed in his possession, yet would he never wholly resign, till he gave it to the beast in Christian Rome, so-called.

On Revelation xiii. 1 Mr. Wesley comments in a way to show that he understood the whole spirit and purpose of the papacy to antedate Christianity. Says he:

Babylon is Rome. All things which the Revelation says of Babylon, agree to Rome, and Rome only. It commenced Babylon when it commenced the Great. When Babylon sunk in the East it rose in the West. And it existed in the time of the apostles, whose judgment is said to be avenged on her. The beast reigns both before and after the reign of Babylon. First, the beast reigns (xiii. 1), then Babylon (xvii. 1), and then the beast again (xvii. 8, etc.).

Babylon was on the decline several centuries before Christ; its temple services ceased about B.C. 29 (Augustus Cæsar reorganized the Roman Empire 27 B.C.); by the end of the first century Babylon was practically dead. On the cessation of temple worship in Babylon emperor worship began in Rome. Wesley and many others have understood the "Babylon" of Revelation to mean the city of Rome. No doubt the apostle John regarded pagan Rome as the true successor of pagan Babylon. It is interesting to note that the Jews who were in intimate contact with Assyrian Babylon were driven to the bitterest hatred of idolatry, just as the Christians were forced by Babylon's successor, Rome, to the profoundest opposition to idolatry, magic, and bloodshed. As the Jews resisted ancient Babylon, so have the Christians resisted modern Babylon. As ancient Babylon persecuted the Jews, so has modern Babylon persecuted the Christians. When Rome, the successor of ancient

Babylon, changed her name and so usurped the name of Christian, she continued the persecution of Christians, with this difference, that she has been more fierce and unrelenting than ever was seen in the history of paganism. Wesley, on Revelation xvii. 4–6, observes:

And the woman was arrayed—With the utmost pomp and magnificence, *in purple and scarlet*—These were the colors of the imperial habit; the purple in times of peace, and the scarlet in times of war, *having in her hand a golden cup*—Like the ancient Babylon (Jer. li. 7), *full of abominations*—The most abominable doctrines as well as practices. *And on her forehead a name written*—Whereas the saints have the name of God and the Lamb on their foreheads. *Mystery*—This very word was insribed on the front of the pope's mitre, till some of the reformers took public notice of it. *Babylon the great . . . the mother of harlots*—The parent, ringleader, patroness, and nourisher of many daughters that closely copy after her; and *abominations*—Of every kind, spiritual and fleshly, *of the earth*—In all lands. In this respect she is indeed catholic or universal. *And I saw the woman drunk with the blood of the saints*—So that Rome may well be called, *The slaughter house of the martyrs.* She hath shed much Christian blood in every age; but at length she is even drunk with it.

Mr. Wesley has no time for trimming. Referring to Revelation xviii. 24, "And in her was found the blood of prophets, and saints, and of all that had been slain upon the earth," he has this to say:

There is no city under the sun which has so clear a title to bloodguiltiness as Rome. The guilt of the blood shed under the heathen emperors has not been removed under the popes, but hugely multiplied. Nor is Rome accountable only for that which hath been shed in the city, but for that shed in all the earth. For at Rome, under the pope, as well as under the heathen emperors, were the bloody orders and edicts given; and wherever the blood of holy men was shed, there were the grand rejoicings for it. And what immense quantities of blood have been shed by her agents! Charles IX. of France, in his letter to Gregory XIII., boasts that in, and not long after, the massacre of Paris, he had destroyed seventy thousand Huguenots. Some have computed that from the year 1518 to 1548 fifteen millions of Protestants have perished by war and the Inquisition! This may be overcharged; but certainly the number of them in those thirty years, as well as since, is almost incredible. To these we may add innumerable martyrs, in ancient, middle, and late ages, in Bohemia, Germany, Holland, France, England, Ireland, and many other parts of Europe, Africa, and Asia.

John Wesley, in his Journal, is also very clear-cut:

The Church of Rome, in its present form, was not founded by Christ himself. All the doctrines and practices wherein she differs from us were not instituted by Christ; they were unknown to the ancient Church of Christ; they are unscriptural, novel corruptions. . . . The generality of its members are no holier than Turks or heathens. . . . Look at the Romanists in London or Dublin; are these the holy, the only holy Church? Just such holiness is in the bottomless pit. (Vol. III., page 42.)

I read Mr. Baxter's History of the Councils. It is utterly astonishing, and would be wholly incredible, but that his vouchers are beyond all exception. What company of execrable wretches have they been . . . who have almost in every age since St. Cyprian taken upon them to govern the Church? How has one Council been perpetually cursing another; and delivering all over to Satan, whether predecessors or contemporaries, who did not implicitly receive their determinations, though generally trifling, sometimes false, and frequently unintelligible or self-contradictory? Surely Mahometanism was let loose to reform the Christians. I know not but Constantinople has gained by the change. (Vol. II., page 281.)

My fragments of time I employed in reading, and carefully considering, the lives of Magdalen de Pazzi and some other eminent Romish saints. I could not but observe: (1) That many things related therein are highly improbable. I fear the relators did not scruple lying for the Church, or for the credit of their order. (2) That many of their reputed virtues were really no virtues at all; being no fruits of the love of God or man, and no part of the mind which was in Christ Jesus. (3) That many of their applauded actions were neither commendable, nor imitable. (4) That what was really good in their tempers or lives was so deeply tinctured with enthusiasm, that most readers would be far more likely to receive hurt than good from these accounts of them. (Vol. III., page 123.)

In my Journal, August 27, 1739, I wrote to a priest that no Romanist, as such, can expect to be saved, according to the terms of the Christian covenant. (Vol. III., page 356.)

The letter of Wesley to the priest is found in Volume I, page 220.

A large house was taken, . . . which receives all the children that come, sometimes above four hundred at once. They are taught gratis, reading, writing, and popery. (Vol. IV., page 119.)

Franz Cumont, one of the most eminent modern authorities on Comparative Religion, has worked out thoroughly the history of old Romanism and has reached the conclusion, in a most scientific manner, that its life, its power, its sentiment, and its efficient organization came from the Orient. Says he:

In whatever direction scholars of to-day pursue their investigations they always notice Asiatic culture supplanting that of Italy. The latter developed only by absorbing elements taken from the inexhaustible reserves of the "old civilizations." [5]

In all the evolutions and changes which have entered into Romanism, before and after the Christian era, there is one stubborn element which remains precisely the same; that is, *the primacy of the State, its superiority over conscience, its control over the re-*

[5] "Oriental Religions in Roman Paganism," 1911.

ligious life, and *its usurpation of God and religion. The Roman Catholic Church is simply the State with religious functions; the pope is nothing more nor less than the emperor with supreme authority also to prescribe the rites and ceremonies and the dogma; the priesthood is the extension of the secular power of the pontiff with spiritual weapons to whip derelicts into line.* While this Italian principle has ever remained central, yet the religions of the East introduced a new frenzy which made the Roman Catholic much more anxious to exterminate his enemies than the old cool-headed Roman would have done. On the one hand, the fiery temper of the Oriental was absorbed into old Romanism; on the other hand, the East would have given to it a better notion of the personal responsibility of the soul to his God, but this the Italians could not assimilate. Papalism has become worse than it might have been by rejecting a better ethical system; it became worse than it was originally by taking on the emotionalism of the cults of Egypt, Assyria, Babylonia, Syria, etc.

Says Cumont:

Perhaps there never was a religion so cold and prosaic as the [old] Roman. Being subordinated to politics, it sought, above all, to secure the protection of the gods for the State and to avert the effects of their malevolence by the strict execution of appropriate practices. . . . The pontiffs, who were also magistrates, regulated the religious practices with the exact precision of jurists. . . . Lacking the recognized authority of official creeds, the Oriental religions had to appeal to the passions of the individual in order to make proselytes. . . . Even the gods, with whom the believers thought they were uniting themselves in their mystic outbursts, were more human and sometimes more sensual than those of the Occident.

The power of the priest was greatly enhanced by the infiltration of Oriental cults. "It was the priests' prerogative to judge the misdeeds and to impose the penalties."

Papal Paganism is an effort to take from mankind the right of access to God and place all such matters in the hands of the State. Along with the Eastern paganism, which brought with it other concepts, came the germ of the confessional, which meant merely a larger secular power under the guise of the spiritual.

The awe-inspiring scenes depicted in the book of Revelation represent scientifically the coming of the dragon from Babylon and the transfer of his cruel power to the Roman Catholic beast.

The strange infatuation which moves Protestants to defend or condone in Romanism things which they would not excuse for an instant in any Evangelical Church is evidence that the religion of Christ must expect great and artful foes to make terrible war on the plain tenets given us by the Man of Galilee. How is it possible for any real follower of Christ not to see the utterly anti-Christian character of Romanism?

It is not necessary to interpret certain prophecies of Scripture as if the writers had specifically in mind the rise and sway of Romanism, but it is certain that Romanism must be included wherever she fulfills the conditions. Other world powers answer to certain descriptions of desperate enmity to the spiritual and pure religion of Jesus, but this does not preclude us from applying these Scriptures also to Rome.

In 2 Thessalonians ii. 3, 4, the "man of sin" is set forth as a *deceiver*, opposing and exalting himself to all that is called God. In Revelation xiii. 14 the second beast is said to *deceive* "them that dwell on the earth."

How can we explain the glaring inconsistency of Christians who condone in Romanism that which they would not tolerate anywhere in Protestantism, except on the principle that they have allowed themselves to be deceived?

Let us notice a few plain facts. Of all the foes to be met by Christian missionaries, none are more bitter, more unscrupulous, or more unrelenting than Catholic priests. On every hand the missionary meets not only the sinful practices taught, cultivated, and exemplified by the Catholic clergy, but he discovers a blind hatred of Christian truth which forces him to expose the secrets of Romish iniquity at the very beginning of his efforts. Even the so-called means of grace only aggravate the evil. All the seven magical sacraments are mere heathen substitutes for grace and morals. The doctrines of the Church are worm-eaten. Submission to the priesthood shuts the devotees off from the truth. That bigotry which is inculcated by priests even in the hearts of tender children leads to an insane hatred of Christians and even of the Christ of the New Testament.

Institutions are somewhat analogous to an organism; when their life has really begun, there is at the center a germinal principle. This vital seat of life can never be changed; whatever modification may come to a religion which has well started on its way is only a development. It is impossible for a plant, an animal, or a religion to return to its beginning and evolve in a different manner.

Buddhism is organized around the principle of *Karma*, the doctrine of the deed. There is no place for mercy, forgiveness, or regeneration. Buddhists may change; Buddhism cannot.

Mormonism is founded on lust. It is a narrow cult with a small outlook, a very short history—young enough withal to make considerable change. But if polygamy is left out, as it has been in one branch, there is no more demand for Mormonism.

Mohammedanism is founded on an unscrupulous god. To exchange their Allah for a reasonable deity or to neglect him and select a better god would be to go back on all history. This they will never do.

Judaism is built on the doctrine of an ethical Supreme Being; it has stood for a long time, its modifications have been great, but it is not changed at heart. It cannot change. It sometimes lapsed into magic in its earlier stages, but that was never vital; prophetism was the germinal principle. The prophet was one who taught and practiced righteousness. Unless Judaism regards Christianity as a development of the religion of Moses, it can never change.

Christianity is based on a spiritual, ethical, merciful God who takes his disciples into fellowship with himself and lays on them the responsibility of giving, by their thought and influence, the love and knowledge of God to the whole world.

The germinal principle of Romanism is magic in the hands of the priest, who seeks to save souls from a Catholic hell, a Catholic *Limbus Infantum*, and a Catholic purgatory, to a Catholic heaven, and who gets a livelihood out of it. Ungodly ambition inspires the priesthood and superstition furnishes the raw material on which it operates.

ROMANISM OPPOSED TO THE TEN COMMANDMENTS

1. The Catholic religion has placed a shabby god in the seat of the Almighty. She has also surrounded him with a lot of subalterns who do not help, but rather aggravate the sin.

2. The only commandment upon which Moses commented immediately after the ten were given is that of *idolatry*. Certainly he thought it was most easily and most likely to be broken. It is the only law in the Decalogue which has the frightful penalty immediately attached of following the descendants of the sinner in order to punish them. Only the mercy of God can save them from it. There is no way for Romanism to escape the charge of idolatry.

3. Every pope who curses the people of God takes the name of God in vain, and all the popes do it. By subscribing to the decrees and canons of the Council of Trent, Catholics generally take God's name in vain; that Council was "full of cursings and bitterness." All true Catholics must follow the immoral instructions of Liguori. In his sanction of perjury, he authorizes all Catholics to swear falsely and profanely. No wonder that the average Catholic man swears. So bad was it that some time ago, to save their face, Romish leaders organized what they termed a "holy name society." That is, one may be a Catholic and swear, but he has the privilege of quitting it if he so desires, on joining said society.

4. Romanism vitiates the Sabbath by making it a day of taboo. One must go to Mass; then he is free

11

to do almost anything he may wish. Wherever Catholics or non-Christians have established the custom, the good Catholic may do servile work on Sunday. In real Romish countries the catechisms teach the people that Saints' days are superior to Sunday; this is done by changing the command, "Remember the Sabbath day, to keep it holy," so that it reads, "Remember to sanctify the feasts." In such countries Sabbath desecration is almost universal, except for the Protestants who live there; at the same time feast days are so frequent that the secular governments have to limit them in order to prevent universal idleness and poverty. (See Ezek. xxii. 26.) The breakdown in Sabbath observance in Protestant countries is no doubt largely due to the laxity of Romanism in this respect.

5. Priests, by meddling in home affairs, alienate husbands from wives, make spies of children, exalt themselves above father and mother, deprive the children and their parents of the use of the Bible, and, by making the Church, rather than the home, central, train children to dishonor father and mother.

6. After murdering hundreds of thousands, the Church of Rome still holds to the doctrine of the murder of heretics.

7. Adultery is caused by the confessional, occasioned by high-priced spurious matrimonial grace, and licensed by the pope where he grants a dispensation for a brother and a sister to marry each other.

8. Rome authorizes and encourages theft when she sanctions gambling, lotteries, betting, secret compensation, short weights and measures. It is also about the same as stealing, if not worse, to take

money for that flummery which priests use in their pretense to get souls out of the nether world.

9. The false witness borne by Romanists against Christians, especially in Catholic countries, is so notorious that it becomes ridiculous.

10. That priests covet the wives and goods of their neighbors is so well known in all Catholic countries that husbands and fathers keep continually on their guard, while governments stop the priests by law from building up great religious fortunes to the detriment of the State. The conditions we discovered in the Philippines bear out these assertions.

Romanism is rebuked by various moral precepts of the Old Testament.

"Thou desirest truth in the inward parts" (Ps. li. 6) is a direct rebuke of the doctrine of mental restriction.

"Divers weights and divers measures, both of them alike are an abomination to the Lord" (Prov. xx. 10), and a terrible arraignment of the Catholic doctrine of short weights and measures.

"Righteousness exalteth a nation; but sin is a reproach to any people" (Prov. xiv. 34), is a withering condemnation of Romish rule in Catholic lands.

"My son, if sinners entice thee, consent thou not. If they say, Come with us, let us lay wait for blood, let us lurk privily for the innocent without cause; . . . we shall find all precious substance, we shall fill our houses with spoil; thou shalt cast thy lot among us; we will all have one purse; my son, walk not thou in the way with them" (Prov. i. 10–15). That is an exact description and a severe condemnation of the robbery and bloodshed practiced by the leaders of the Romish Church during several hundred years. The Inquisition was a pretext to get the money and goods of the better class of citizens; it was easier to kill them and take their gold than it was to work and earn it.

Romanism is an enemy of the Old Testament in that she misinterprets it, and even then, where it is possible, keeps it out of the hands of the people. No book in the world is so terrific in its condemnation of idolatry as is the Old Testament; the difference between the idolatry assaulted by Moses and the prophets and that practiced by Romanists cannot be explained away by the hierarchy. The puerility of some Romish notes is equally incorrect. The comment in the Douay Bible on Tobias xi. 9 is a sample of Romish scholarship. The verse reads: "Then the dog, which had been with them in the way, ran before, and coming as if he had brought the news, showed his joy by his fawning and wagging his tail." Catholic comment: "Here in the mystical sense are represented to us God's holy preachers, who bring us the good tidings of salvation." If it suits a Catholic priest to be represented by a dog who shows his joy by "fawning and wagging his tail," that is his privilege; to Protestant preachers the Romish exposition is not only incorrect, but ludicrous.

Romanism is further removed from New Testament principles than from those of the Old Testament. If Catholicism had always known little or nothing of the Christian religion, it is conceivable that she might hold all the things inherent in Romanism and be only non-Christian. While her life was of a different origin from that of the Christian religion, yet she has been in intimate contact with her great rival, as manifested in the different sects, for fifteen centuries. Romanism, unlike Judaism, has always been exceedingly hostile to Christianity, because, unlike Judaism, she has pretended to be identical with the religion of Christ.

Romanism has rejected Christ by attributing to him the authority for her immoral casuistry, by cursing millions whom he has blessed, and by denying to his people access to his teachings.

She has rejected the atonement of Christ by pretending to offer him as a sacrifice every time she celebrates the Mass.

Romanism has usurped Christ's authority by granting the pope the right to absolve subjects from their oath of allegiance to governments. This gives him the right to authorize perjury, something the Master never taught.

Romanism is built on principles antagonistic to the Beatitudes (Matt. v. 1–12). "Blessed are the poor in spirit," says Jesus. By no sort of interpretation can the pope, the cardinals, the archbishops, the bishops, or even the ordinary priests be called poor in spirit. Instead of mourning in any good cause, Romish priests cause others to mourn. The Catholic hierarchy would like to inherit the earth, but only the meek shall enjoy that privilege. The hierarchy, on account of their ambitions, have steadily lost their earthly inheritance; that explains the whimpering of the popes that they are "prisoners of the Vatican." Romish priests hunger and thirst for power, but not for righteousness. Instead of mercy,

Romish priests practice cursing, favoritism, injustice, and the persecution of men who have convictions and who follow those convictions. Jesus taught that the pure in heart should see God; Rome teaches that those who pretend to believe the Creed, who submit to their legitimate pastors, and partake of the sacraments shall probably see God, if the officiating priests have had the right intention. Jesus came to bring peace, and he proclaimed as children of God all peacemakers; the Romish clergy are incurable mischiefmakers. Christ congratulates those who suffer persecution for righteousness' sake; Rome congratulates those who persecute righteous men. If the reader doubts this, let him try to practice and publicly recommend the pure principles of Jesus in any Catholic country. It is not the simple precepts of Christ which Rome pretends to defend in her persecutions; it is her whole system of innovations for which she fights.

Romanism cannot change radically without giving to her members the right of private interpretation of Scripture. This would destroy the *mechanical* unity of the Church as it fortunately has done among Protestants. Romanists could not be delivered to that sort of a *régime*. Any alteration which does not include the right of private interpretation would not be a radical change; it would only be a slight modification. This right cannot be granted, for many reasons. The body of the Church would then call for a digest of the great mass of traditions with which an attempt would be made to harmonize the Bible. Such Catholics would pry into the secrets of the "Unanimous consent of the fathers," about which they had heard so much and which had been kept sacred for centuries, so sacred that unordained hands had no right to touch it. They would throw overboard the lying comments which had formerly neutralized the scathing Scripture rebukes of idolatry.

The Roman Catholic religion is made to rest on four pillars; suppose we call them house-blocks. They are called the "four notes of the Church." These are called *unity, sanctity, apostolicity, and catholicity.* Only one of these "notes" is worth considering: that is, *sanctity.* The other three are subsidiary to it. We do not desire nor fear *universality* (catholicity) if the religion is unholy. If it is unholy, it is not *apostolic;* the apostles did not teach unholy doctrine. Its *unity* we grant; that is the shame of Romanism, and, strange to say, she glories in her shame.

The so-called holiness of Rome consists in her magical sacraments, which foster fanaticism but not righteousness; her teachings, which are hopelessly unethical; her saints, some of whom were the greatest monsters of iniquity.

If the unholy teachings of the Church should be denounced, that would not save her at this late date. The venerable casuist (Liguori) who finally settled those evils on the Church was duly studied by the theologians, and authoritatively recommended for canonization by the Sacred Congregation for the Beatification and Canonization of Saints. At the proper time, the reigning pope constituted him a saint. Now he is in, and "all the king's horses can't pull him out;" as well try to pull a hole out of the ground. To fill up the hole so that he could crawl

out of his farcical holiness would be to impeach the
theology of the theologians, the sacredness and
authority of the Sacred Congregation, and, finally,
the primacy of the pope. That would be to unsaint
a saint; if one such could be uncanonized, then no
Romish saint is safe in his "holy" eminence.

The holiness corner is the main corner of the Catholic edifice; in that portion of the building are to be
found the confessional box, the altar, the pulpit,
and the choir. Above these are the tower, the belfry,
and the chimes. When the block under that corner
rots, the building may stand awry for a while, but it
must finally fall; and great will be the fall thereof.
Meanwhile the pulpit has lost its authority, the confessional its certainty, the altar its sacredness, the
choir its harmony, the tower its prominence, the bell
its blessing, and the chimes their joy.

Romanism is in a terrible dilemma. If she stands
by Liguori, she remains as ever an enemy of Jesus
Christ, she continues to fight against the moral progress of the nations, she proclaims her innate love of
iniquity, and she gnashes her teeth at the onward
march of Protestant Christianity. If she repudiates
Liguori, she digs the ground from under her feet, for
her strength consists in her harmony with such out-
rageously artful "doctors" as he.

THE NATURE OF ROMANISM IS THAT OF A PARASITE

A parasite cannot live by itself; it must have a host.
The Catholic Church always degenerates when left
alone; it carries within itself the seeds of decay.

The parasite flourishes in proportion to the vigor of
its host. All prosperous countries owe their greatness

precisely to those principles which are condemned by Romanism—*e. g.*, freedom of the press, of worship, of conscience, separation of Church and State, and education by the State.

The parasite shows no care for the life of the host.

England has protected and nourished Ireland and Quebec. The United States has given Catholics freedom of worship. Mexico has allowed Roman priests all the liberty she has dared to grant them. Yet Ireland hates England, the hierarchy in the United States despises our freedom, and Mexico has been systematically slandered by the hierarchy ever since the terrible curses fulminated against her by Pius IX. when she threw off the Romish yoke.

The tendency of the parasite is gradually to kill the host. Rome succeeded in that policy in Spain and Austria. Italy and France suppressed the parasite to some extent, and this has been of immense help to those countries.

The death of the host brings the death or else the emigration of the parasite. To keep from dying in Italy, Austria, and Spain, Romanism over a hundred years ago began to look for a fresh, vigorous host on which to feed. She found it principally in the New World. Now that Latin America is ready to throw her off, she is giving special attention to the United States and England.

The repression of the parasite is necessary for its own life. The best friends of the Catholic Church are those who will not let her have her own way. The United States has made Romanism far more respectable than she ever has been in Mexico, Peru, Bolivia, Ecuador, Spain, or the West Indies. If the Romish

Church had to depend entirely on the type of religionists produced exclusively by her own life and doctrines, she could hardly survive another generation.

The most vigorous life of the host is impossible without the elimination of the parasite. The Roman Catholic religion is an anachronism in the twentieth century; she is strangely out of place. She is "like a broken tooth or a foot out of joint."

Romanism is not simply anti-Christian, but maliciously anti-Christian. Since the beginning of the "venomous period" (A.D. 1870) she has reasserted those instincts which animated the people during the days of Julius Cæsar when "the high society of Rome itself became a society of powerful animals with an enormous appetite for pleasure," when "to make money—money by any means, lawful or unlawful—became the universal passion." It is not primarily the destruction of Protestantism which Rome seeks. The Christian religion is the only formidable obstacle in her way; Christianity is therefore the main object of attack. Romanism seeks her own glory and power; Christianity seeks righteousness and peace. We need not, however, fear Romish wealth so much as Romish intrigue, by which the wealth of unsuspecting non-Catholics is used for purposes of corruption. Romanism is a plunderer. When the world was wild, she plundered with comparative ease. Peace, science, universal education, a spiritual religion, justice, and democracy drive out superstition, idolatry, and hypocrisy. This makes the task of establishing Christianity in the face of Romish hatred and intrigue much more hopeful than ever before.

CHAPTER VI

CHRISTIANITY THE ONLY ANTIDOTE

THE Roman question must be met and settled. There are three wrong ways of looking at the matter: (1) We may take the position that the mass of Romanists are indifferent or superficial in their loyalty to the pope and the unchanging tenets of their religion; (2) we may decide that, since Romanism is what it is, we may as well let it alone and ask Catholics to let us alone; (3) we might conclude that, since Romanism claims supremacy over civil government, Protestants would better change their doctrine and assume full authority over the State just as Rome has done.

There is no reason to accept the first of these positions; Romanists are not indifferent. The notion that the "holy father" is supreme in civil affairs is held by enough Catholics to make it a knotty problem. All who are thoroughly instructed by the priests and sisters and nuns, all who are taught in parochial schools, all who are under the full dominance of the priests, have drunk in the virus of Romanism until they are intoxicated with it. They have received a peculiar twist which is almost impossible for a Protestant or liberal to understand.

To let Romanism and Romanists alone is utterly impossible; if the cult were not essentially aggressive and domineering in the political realm, we might fight it out from the pulpit and through the Church press. Catholics cannot let others alone and be true to their fundamentals.

(171)

Suppose we should decide to adopt Romish methods, requiring all non-Protestant religions to cease from public worship in Protestant countries. The very fact that we do not and cannot conscientiously undertake such a barbarous thing is pointed out by Romanists as a sign of weakness. We are ridiculed as having no real convictions because we are liberal toward all cults, though of course faithful to our own religion. If we could and should try to assert the supremacy of Protestantism in civil government, there would necessarily be a war of extermination. Such a thought should put Romanists to shame. Why have we not the same right that they claim? We are not contending for the thing which is the basic animus of Rome. Catholic theologians show their perfidy at this point.

Every Catholic is expected to "reject, condemn, and anathematize" everything contrary to his "faith," while it is a mortal sin for him to study those things which he curses. His theologians contend that if a Protestant should condemn Romanism without studying it from Catholic sources he would be dishonest. On the other hand, Catholics are so far above the ordinary laws of honesty and decency that they are not only permitted, but required, to condemn what they do not understand.

Protestants must not do mission work in Catholic countries, while Catholics must convert all Protestants if they can.

Protestants are expected to recognize as divine a marriage performed by a priest and to respect those who are thus married. Catholics are required to calumniate those who, having been baptized in the

Catholic Church, are married without the priest. They must hold that the children of such marriages are illegitimate.

Protestants are expected to respect a Protestant who forsakes his Church and joins a Catholic Church. Catholics are taught that whoever leaves the Romish fold and joins an Evangelical Church is a hypocrite.

A Catholic holds that he may maliciously oppose the Constitution of the United States in so far as that document prescribes separation of Church and State, freedom of worship for non-Catholics, freedom of the press, and freedom of conscience. A Protestant who upholds the Constitution as against this un-American doctrine is branded as intolerant.

A Catholic must hold that there is no salvation outside of the Catholic Church except in the case of invincible ignorance. The Protestant who holds that he may be a Christian and with full knowledge reject the iniquities and idolatries of Romanism is regarded by "strong Catholics" as bigoted.

A Catholic is required to boycott a heretic. Suppose this method should be followed by all non-Catholic religions. Whenever Protestants undertake to defend themselves against Catholic boycott they are immediately branded as being unfair.

Protestants contend that all religions should have equal rights before the law; Romanists contend that they should have special protection from the civil government.

But the Catholic question is not simply national; it is also international. Protestants must decide whether or not we are to preach and teach our own doctrines fearlessly. It is impossible and unscriptural to confine our efforts to setting forth our tenets without exposing the inherent errors and evils of anti-Christian religions. If we would promote the nations, the governments, the business interests, the social life of the world, we must help them to discern the basic difference between the religion of Christ, which is primarily spiritual, and the Catholic religion, which is first of all political.

On every hand the religion of Italy is in deadly conflict with the prophetic religion which was born in Palestine and promulgated by Jesus Christ. The arena of this struggle covers the globe. When we undertake to meet the religions of China, we are there dealing with certain varieties of cults whose fullest expression took their form and reached their perfection in Rome. In India or Africa it is the same. The eternal difference between Christianity and all other religions can never be made plain until we recognize the unfathomable abyss there is between Christianity and Romanism.

WORLD-WIDE MISSIONS AND ROMANISM

Now that Roman Catholic Europe has become a special field for Protestant missionary operations, we must give our reasons so clearly that all our Protestant constituency can know exactly why we have undertaken such a task. For a hundred years we have also been meeting the Roman question in Latin America, in various parts of Europe, and in all other mission fields of the world.

Romanism is either Christian or it is not. If it is Christian at heart, then it becomes our duty to help the hierarchy to remove the excrescences; if it is not

Christian, we are under obligation to show that it is not.

The burning question of aggressive Christianity everywhere is how to deal with priestcraft. Practically all non-Christian religions are based on the power of magic to placate capricious gods. The main manipulators of magic are the priests. Whether it be Mohammedan imams, or the medicine-men of the Redskins, or the voodoo doctors of Africa, or the priests of Buddhism, Taoism, and Brahmanism, or the hierarchy of Romanism, it is all one. Under the protection of these go-betweens, whose business it is to stand between angry gods and erring men, all sorts of sin and misfortunes flourish. All classes of priests, when unchecked by a higher morality, place ritual above ethics; even when impeded by the better elements of society there is always conflict.

It is not mere human weakness or perversity or ignorance with which the Christian religion must cope. The greatest barrier to the spiritual and ethical message of Christianity is always some other religion or philosophy which has preëmpted the territory. Virtually all non-Christian cults are principally occupied with innumerable laws and ceremonies; this makes the priesthood indispensable. Any effort to introduce a purely spiritual religion is at once regarded as an effort to wrest the people from the grasp of those who invent and authorize the minutiæ of conduct and of hocus-pocus. The secret hatred of the Pharisees, the scribes, and the priests for Jesus Christ was that his simple religion made their elaborate services unnecessary. This is still the animus of the virulent opposition to the religion of the Nazarene.

Of all the non-Christian faiths in the world to-day, there is none so well organized, so thoroughly aggressive, so insinuating, or so effective as is the Roman Catholic religion. We shall never be fully equipped for offering to the world the pure religion of Jesus Christ until we define our attitude to Romanism. As long as we continue to dally with that question we shall fail to present a solid front to the world.

Whatever good there is in Romanism is due to extraneous influences. She is a corrupt tree, and "a corrupt tree cannot bring forth good fruit." The Vatican decree which pronounced the pope to be infallible crowned the system as a religion of priests. Jesus has accurately described that sort of leaders: "Verily, verily, I say unto you, He that entereth not by the door into the fold of the sheep, but climbeth up some other way, the same is a thief and a robber. . . . The thief cometh not, but that he may steal, and kill, and destroy." (John x. 1, 10.)

Catholicism to-day is practically Jesuitism. It was the unscrupulous followers of Loyola who brought about the Counter Reformation. They were so entirely Roman Catholic that several of their own popes were terrified when they saw in them as in a mirror the exact image of their own Romish characters. Afterwards the Jesuits were first endured, then pitied, and then embraced. Their diabolical scheme was well laid. The theory of Jesuitic casuistry had been slowly developed; then it went through the alembic of Liguori's brain. After the teaching department of the Church reflected profoundly on it they accepted it for all time. Even if Catholic dogma were Christian, the virulent immorality which has impregnated her entire system would vitiate all her theology. Morality cannot take first place in any genuinely ritualistic religion. But that is not all; morality must sooner or later be regarded as a rival of a religion based on ceremonialism. We have a concrete case of this in Mexico to-day. The nobler elements of society there are now trying to eliminate gambling; but in this they must fight the influence of the priests and the doctrines of Romish theologians.

Several helpful remedies have been used to cure the sin of Romanism. All have helped, but only Christianity may be considered as a specific. The *schisms* of the Greek Church and of the Old Catholic Church have been of considerable benefit. *Liberalism* and *Agnosticism* have to some extent arrested the deterioration of Romanism, notably in France and Latin America; but they have not proven vigorous enough. They usually grant that the Catholic religion would be tolerable if practiced in its purity; forgetting that, as with poison, the purer it is the more deadly it becomes. *Masonry* had much to do with driving the French out of Mexico, ignoring the blessing which Pius IX. had so recklessly bestowed on Maximilian. *Good government,* as long as it maintains self-respect, checkmates priestly meddling. But there is a continual breaking down of moral integrity among politicians unless they are powerfully braced up by individual and organized Christianity. Even in the United States right now the doctrine of the separation of Church and State is being weakened. Corrupt politicians permit the government to make large grants of money to Catholic schools, hospitals, and eleemosynary institu-

12

tions. *General education, the press, public libraries,* and *the march of science* are great agencies if they will only function. But the public schools of this country allow their medieval histories to be viciously twisted in order to please the Jesuits. The press—except the anti-Catholic and in some cases the religious— trembles in the presence of Romish threats much as a rabbit would in the presence of a bulldog. Romanists are the only set of people who successfully defy news-papers to print their authorized doctrines. Public libraries are closely censored. The findings of science, if brought to bear on Romish magic, would make it absurd; little of this is done.

1. WITH WHOM DO WE DEAL?

1. *Catholics in all the world.* Not all Romanists are on a dead level; there are several species.

(1) *Good Catholics.* This species is subdivided into two strains. (a) Good Catholics, but shabby Chris-tians, are those who barely suspect the iniquities of their religion. These constitute perhaps fifty per cent; more in Catholic countries, less in Protestant lands. Many of these are dissatisfied, but know not where to go. On the humility and rectitude of many of these depends the success of Romanism while she tries to live in the blaze of twientieth-century light. They are poor Christians, for they must know that their Church is a sworn enemy to all efforts of Protes-tants to free the nations from strong drink, gambling, illiteracy, and the social evil. (b) Good Catholics who know something of the perfidy of Romanism, but who honestly believe that no religion can be any bet-ter. The priests have succeeded in convincing some

of their intelligent members and nearly all of the ignorant ones that if Romanism is not the only form of Christianity, then there is no Christianity. Many submit to their fate and remain in what they regard as a very imperfect Church because they know little or nothing of any other. Some of these are Christians because their own consciences have led them to an appreciation of a few Christian principles, which they have learned here and there despite the Machiavellianism of their official religion. But it cannot be said that they are of much use in the world while they stand aloof from the great moral movements of their own times.

(2) *Strong Catholics.* These are a belligerent class. They are trained to show fierce anger at any exposure of Romish turpitude. "Theirs not to reason why; theirs but to do and [spiritually] die." A "strong Catholic" is not one who has strong convictions of religious truth, but one who has strong prejudices. With a strange blindness the strong Catholic fiercely defends his right to know nothing of the inner doctrines of his own Church.

(3) *Practical Catholics.* These are practical infidels. They would as readily be practical Mohammedans, or practical Christians, or anything else that is sufficiently practical to bring shekels to themselves and social recognition to their wives and daughters. Every Knight of Columbus who refuses to go to confessional, or to let his family go, is a practical Catholic. Like the unjust judge, he "fears not God." Unlike said judge, he does regard man, but in a most ungodly and timeserving manner.

(4) *The priesthood.* These are the ones who "make

the wheels go 'round." (a) The lower clergy is only theoretically separated from the membership; its ignorance makes it pliable and obedient. (b) The higher clergy includes the ones who manipulate their fellow priests and other classes in the Church, to say nothing of many outside its membership. These are they who "set at naught dominion, and rail at dignities. . . . They went in the way of Cain, and ran riotously in the way of Balaam for hire. . . . Shepherds that without fear feed themselves; clouds without water, . . . autumn trees without fruit. . . . These are murmurers, complainers, walking after their lusts (and their mouth speaketh great swelling words), showing respect of persons for the sake of advantage. . . . These are they who make separations, sensual, having not the Spirit. (Jude.) Seldom are members of the higher clergy converted. Jude says of this class: "On some have mercy, who are in doubt; and some save, snatching them out of the fire; and on some have mercy with fear; hating even the garment spotted by the flesh."

The main feature of the sacerdotal program for the exploitation of their people is to form a buffer class out of all the species we have mentioned. Time-serving Protestants are also utilized as members of the buffer class. In a monarchy, a coterie of nobles is necessary; in a democracy, such societies as the Knights of Columbus, sodalities, sisters of charity, etc., are indispensable. Everywhere there must be an educated caste and a number of fanatical and wealthy women.

(5) *Discontented, nominal, and indifferent Catholics.* These partially overlap the first class; they

form about three-fourths of the population of all Catholic countries. This seventy-five per cent of the population of Catholic Europe are extending a hand of welcome to Protestants now.

Our great hope in missionary work among Romanists is that so many of them are not so familiar with the real tenets of their Church as to be entirely and hopelessly debauched by their vicious religion.

2. *Protestants in Catholic countries.* These have borne the burden and heat of the day in the age-long struggle with Romanism and deserve great sympathy and admiration.

(1) The natives. *The Waldenses,* the "Israel of the Alps," are the *oldest Protestant body in Christendom,* dating back to Peter Waldo, who was born about 1140. When we consider at what frightful cost our freedom was bought and what these Christians have suffered in witnessing to the grace of Christ, we must feel bound to them by the strongest ties of gratitude.

In the heart of *Hungary* there are "two millions and a half of Protestant Magyars with a Protestant fealty of more than four hundred years."

In *France* "the celebration of the Second Centennial of the Revocation in 1885 brought to Protestants the realization that their noble ancestors had not suffered in vain. More than one thousand pastors were preaching; and though there were only six hundred thousand Protestants, these were one hundred and seventy-five thousand more than in 1806. . . . First of all European nations, France had emancipated the human soul; religion had ceased to be a function of government."

Czecho-Slovakia is one of the first-fruits of the

World War. The grace of God has reached these who, instead of being in constant danger of breaking out into war, will probably become as a healing fountain for the European continent. This will certainly be the case if a majority of her population shall discover the futility of priests in order to obtain personal access to the God of peace—the God of all grace.

In *all Catholic countries* will be found a few Protestants who are as the salt of the earth, even if they cannot as yet be as the light of the world.

(2) *The Protestant immigrants into Catholic lands.* These have the same right to live and breathe as other people. But they are denied the right to worship God publicly, except where liberalism interferes; even then the petty persecutions continue.

3. *Free thinkers* who would not be cowed, but have openly broken with the Church. They deserve great credit and help. They have intervened to save their people and have already gained a partial victory.

2. What Is Our Goal?

Nothing less than the elimination of the virus of Romanism can satisfy those who suffer from its malignity. Let us give Romanists exactly that which they lack.

Passing over the questions of idolatry, magic, and purgatory, we may emphasize certain things.

Romanists need a ministry whose efficacy consists in witnessing, teaching, and preaching. It was specifically the prophetic element of the Old Testament which Jesus sought to conserve.

The world is sorely in need of a consistent and practical code of morals. Catholics must be saved from Catholicism in order to be saved from sin. Protestantism has one system of moral conduct. The Federal Council of the Churches of Christ in America has recently published what is known as the Social Creed of the Churches. This is very significant. The creed is practical, comprehensive, and influential. All Protestant Churches unite in accepting the Sermon on the Mount; Romanism does not join us here. She has a code of her own. In the interests of humanity it is the duty of Protestants continually to hold up before the Catholic world the ethics of Jesus.

Separation of Church and State must be maintained as against the Romish view. This implies, in general, the sovereignty of the State. Some of the things embraced in the doctrine of the sovereignty of civil government are:

1. The full right to tax *all* property. This is denied by the Catholic Church.

2. No taxation without representation. That was denied to the people of the States of the Church in Italy before 1870.

3. Trial by jury. The Catholic Inquisition had no such practice.

4. The right of the accused to be brought face to face with the accuser. The infamous Inquisition denied this right, also.

5. Security of private residence against unreasonable search. The Romish government in Italy invaded any house at any time, day or night, when it wished to do so.

6. The presumption that a prisoner is innocent until he is found to be guilty. The Romish government of Italy and the Catholic Inquisition every-

where presumed a prisoner to be guilty until he proved his innocence.

7. That there shall be no establishment of religion. That is diametrically opposed to the *ex-cathedra* and unchangeable teaching of the Romish Church.

8. The sovereign right of the State to educate the youth of the country. This is explicitly denied by the Catholic Church to be the prerogative of the State.

9. The right to protect all citizens and strangers living within its territory. Rome claims the right to arrest escaped nuns and place them back in the nunneries.

10. The authority to determine who may perform the rite of matrimony, also priority in determining for its citizens what are the conditions which make marriage lawful or unlawful. This is condemned by the Syllabus of Errors.

11. Freedom of worship, freedom of the press, freedom of conscience, freedom of thought, freedom of assembly, freedom of speech. All these are forever condemned in an *ex-cathedra* manner by the popes.

For every one of these principles we must contend, not only as Protestants but as citizens. This is the only path to peace and we must have peace if we have to fight for it. He who stands for these principles is not the aggressor in his defense of them.

We must insist on the preservation of national life, including the rights of each individual, instead of its destruction. This is the opposite of Romish ideas and methods. We must steadfastly oppose the civil punishment of heresy. The State must not call into question the religious beliefs of any law-abiding citizen or foreigner within its gates. It cannot be proven that unity of religious belief is essential to the permanence of a nation. Germany, Turkey, and Austria-Hungary each had unity of faith; as much so as governments could secure such unity. Now Germany has declared in favor of separation of Church and State; she has learned the great lesson of the World War. Turkey must make such a declaration before the world can endure her and before she can endure herself.[1] Austria is bankrupt and conditions in Hungary are very little better. Palestine cannot have peace without freedom of worship; England has therefore given it to her. Spain, Peru, Bolivia, and Ecuador, each had unity of belief during the World War. What did these countries contribute to the cause of progress during that great conflict? On the other hand, the United States, the British Empire, Italy, and France had set up as their aim religious freedom of the individual and of the nation rather than the lordship of Romanism or any other religion over the individual conscience. These were the nations that saved the world from a return to the reign of force.

The Bible is the great textbook which inculcates all the principles we have just examined. All Evangelical denominations accept the sixty-six books as we have them; all desire that the book be circulated throughout the world, with or without comment; all believe in the private interpretation of Scripture.

Dr. Yu Yue-tsu, a distinguished Chinese educator,

[1] Turkey has made such a declaration since the above was written.

sent the following cablegram for Bible Day at the Methodist Centenary at Columbus, Ohio, in 1919:

The translation of the Christian Bible into our national language has placed in the hands of our people a book than which there is none with greater power for moral uplift and spiritual enlightenment. The great ideas of divine love, human brotherhood, holiness, unselfish service, all culminating in the wonderful ideal of the kingdom of God on earth, are emphasized and exemplified in its pages as nowhere else. They are powerful dynamics in undoing social wrongs and erasing class distinctions, in humanizing social relationships and democratizing governments. They have condemned the opium traffic, raised the status of women and children, purified the home, emancipated the slaves, energized the moral nature of man, taught the value of human life, produced happiness in life and labor, and created a new conscience both for the individual and the community. The open Bible, the greatest heritage of Christendom, is now made accessible to China's millions, and it will not fail as their guide and inspirer in the nation's upward struggle for moral perfection and spiritual freedom.

Hundreds of quotations could be made from the greatest minds of earth as to the sublimity of the teachings of Holy Scripture. What concerns us here is its *inestimable value in the life of the individual.* The danger of private interpretation, which Romish leaders pretend to fear, is merely the danger that laymen will find in the Bible an infinitely higher code of morals and religion than the theologians of Rome have found there. The private interpretation of laymen has never yet discovered in the Holy Scriptures the Romish doctrines of theft, perjury, and idolatry. The Bible reveals a God without "saints" and images, with whom man can commune. From the Psalms of David to the Apocalypse of St. John, God is shown to be a personal friend. In the olden time God spoke to the pious Jew; in the new age he courteously and tenderly, yet unweariedly, stands at the door and knocks, saying: "If any man hear my voice and open the door, I will come in to him, and sup with him, and he with me" (Rev. iii. 20).

Let us give to our Catholic friends a good God for a bad one; grace instead of magic; a gospel ministry in the place of a priesthood; morality where they have had sin and vice; freedom rather than force; spiritual life and joy where death and despair have reigned. In short, let us, by every means possible, help them attain spiritual life through him who came that "all men might have life, and have it more abundantly."

3. WHAT IS OUR ENCOURAGEMENT?

1. Despite Rome's bitter, unrelenting opposition, Protestantism, from small beginnings, has grown to a mighty army. It has played a leading part in creating the most powerful nations of the world.

2. Romanism has signally failed in countries where she had complete control. Hence every Catholic government hates the Catholic Church. As a result of this failure, the people who have come to understand the situation are willing to try Christianity.

3. Protestantism is making its appeal in non-Christian lands. Romanism is only a feeble rival; she has shown her helplessness as a missionary force. We may group the evils of paganism under ten categories: seven sins and three misfortunes. The sins are: theft, gambling, lying, unchastity, cruelty, laziness, and idolatry. The misfortunes are: ignorance, poverty, and disease. Out of the cardinal sins grow corruption in government, extortion in finance,

greed in business, unhappiness in home life, reaching
finally the level of ignorance, poverty, and disease.

Romanism has never yet helped to remove *theft,
lying, and gambling.* She has inevitably fostered
them because she deliberately sanctions them. *Unchastity* is not lessened by a religion whose priests
degenerate as soon as they are thrown out into the
nations whom they would fain convert. Few Catholics, even, believe that priests are miraculously
kept from falling while they impudently pry into the
secrets of feminine thoughts and practices. How
could Romish missionaries expect pagans gladly to
exchange their own *cruelties* for those of Romanism?
Boycott in business and ostracism in society are
among the milder weapons used by Rome for sub-
duing heretical souls; pagans are not attracted by
that sort of a religion. Where is the benefit to be derived from exchanging pagan indolence for Catholic
laziness? Where is the advantage of swapping one
sort of idolatry for another? Catholic *ignorance,*
Catholic *poverty,* and Catholic *disease* have nothing
particularly attractive about them. If the seven
sins and the three misfortunes which are almost universal in paganism are not removed, or even materially lessened by Romanism, why should any non-
Christian nation welcome Romish missionaries?

4. Protestants have profoundly affected those
Catholics who are scattered among them. Perhaps
more than half of the members of the Romish Church
in the United States are honestly shocked when
brought face to face with the doctrines of their own
Church. That is worth something.

5. Protestantism has been eminently successful

in its missionary work in Catholic countries. This does not always show up in statistics. In all Latin America, for example, there are about one hundred and thirty thousand Protestants; but these few have a profound influence in helping to shape the future policies of those governments. In Italy the progress of Evangelical Missions has been remarkable.

6. The hierarchy fears and hates Protestant missionaries to Catholics. The late Pope Benedict showed his great alarm at the virility of Evangelical Christianity by asking the Catholic world to pray for the failure of Protestant Missions in Europe. He cursed the beneficent work of the Y. M. C. A. because it might lead his people to read the Bible for themselves. Several popes of the nineteenth and twentieth centuries have foamed at the mouth in their ravings against Bible Societies, against Protestant Missions in the city of Rome, against Masonry, and against governments whose authority is derived from the people and not from the Catholic Church.

The hierarchy brands all converts from Romanism to Christianity as hypocrites. If this were true, then the whole Protestant movement was originally founded on hypocrites. It is wonderful what these Protestant scoundrels have done for the good of the race!

Romanism teaches officially that all converts from Rome who have been married without the presence of the priest are living in adultery and that their children are illegitimate. This is a calumny of the blackest dye.

It is the universal doctrine that a convert from Romanism must be boycotted in business; he must be denounced secretly to the hierarchy; he must be denied any assistance either spiritual or material; if he is dying in a Catholic hospital, a Protestant minister must not be called to see him.

Every Catholic in accepting the Creed of Pius IV. must anathematize everything the Church anathematizes. The bull, *In Cœna Domini*, anathematizes all and singular Protestants of every description.

Rome is fighting education by the State as never before. There are three reasons for this: (1) Catholic schools must teach union of Church and State, the superiority of Romanism to the civil government, and the denial of freedom of worship. (2) The doctrines of theft, lying, perjury, fraud, gambling, and the murder of heretics are fundamental doctrines officially sanctioned in Romish schools. (3) The use of images in worship, the power of exorcism to ward off disease, demons, and ill luck, the miracle-working power of images, relics, and of priests are essentials of a Catholic education. These three things find no place in the public schools.

Rome's ways of meeting opposition are interesting. They are: (1) Hide from the people generally all Catholic books which reveal the inner malignity of Romanism. (2) Ignore, as long as possible, all exposures of genuine Roman Catholic diabolism. (3) Deny, pretend to be horrified, evade, appeal to Christian charity, become fiercely angry, whine, raise the cry of "persecution," brand their enemies as "bigots." (4) Bring counter charges on the principle that, if Protestants are as bad as Catholics, it follows that Catholics are better than Protestants. (5) Attack, by personal violence or by slander, any individual who dares to expose Romanism.

7. Protestantism—*i. e.*, evangelical Christianity—is capable of becoming a world religion.

Such a religion must be adapted to increasingly progressive stages of life and thought. This is true of gospel Christianity and, as we have abundantly shown, it is not true anywhere of Romanism.

A world religion must be able to commend its history to the human race. Romanism cannot escape her responsibility in this respect; she has not shown the least sign of repentance for her terribly guilty past. Protestantism admits with regret her mistakes, some of which she inherited from Romanism before she shook off the incubus of that system.

Any philosophy to become universal must accept as fundamental the dignity of the individual. Respect for personality is the secret of true success in dealing with human beings. Magic necessarily denies the capabilities of all those who are outside the magical caste. No mere human can ever hope to enter the class who can create its Maker, forgive the sins of men, and pull souls out of purgatorial fires.

Any applicant for the position of a world religion must present a clean code of morals. For this a printed text must be placed in the hands of all who will receive it. No government in the world would accept the Romish code of morals: the best governments are built on the Protestant system. Protestantism issues annually about thirty-five million Bibles, Testaments, and portions. During a little over one hundred years we have placed fully six hundred million Bibles, Testaments, and portions in the hands of the people throughout the world. The Bible or portions of it have been translated into seven hundred and seventy languages and dialects. This work of translation and distribution is now going on more rapidly than ever before.

A world religion must not be encumbered with an elaborate ritual. Why should a non-Christian cult exchange its ritual for that of Rome? How can it be proven that one set of ceremonies will captivate a capricious god more effectually than would some other forms of flummery? Ethics carries its own credentials; ritual does not.

A universal religion must be able to unite its followers on the essentials. Protestant denominations are united on one God as revealed in the Bible, salvation by faith without penance or meritorious good works, the place of the ministry as composed of pastors and preachers—not as wonder-workers—the separation of Church and State, and the building up of civil government.

4. What Is Our Duty?

1. To know accurately the genuine teachings of Romanism. Ignorance on a matter of that sort is no credit to a Protestant; such ignorance does not lead to charity or pity, but to guilty compromise.

2. If Catholics are to be brought face to face with their responsibility, they must be caused to see the nature and results of their own doctrine and polity. If the iniquities of Romanism are not to be rebuked, then consistency requires that Christians do not rebuke any other kind of paganism or wickedness. If no sin is to be rebuked, then let us abandon our Bibles, for the Holy Scriptures condemn sin of all kinds and instruct the disciples of that Book to do the same.

If we fail in our duty at this point, the blood of men will be upon our heads. As long as priests stir up riots and have non-Catholics arrested and punished because Romish doctrines are being exposed, it is our plain duty to continue all the more earnestly to expose the malicious teachings and tactics of Romanism.

3. To do missionary work among those who have been left torn and bleeding by that ruthless religion.

4. To prevent their leaders from exploiting or intimidating us. When we are urged to send our children to a Catholic school, let us ask certain questions. For example: "Will you teach our children your fundamental doctrines of secret compensation and mental restriction? If you will not, you should so state it in your school catalogues. But if you are to do that, why should you continue your Catholic schools? Why not say openly, 'We shall renounce Catholic morals and teach the ethics of Protestantism?'" Those Catholic schools that bid for Protestant children should respect our Bible or say that they do not. Is the doctrine of mental restriction practiced when we are told that nothing will be done to interfere with the religion of our children? When we have servant girls in our houses, let us remember that if they are faithful Catholics it is their duty to report to their confessor whatever matters he may wish to know; the same may be said of typists and secretaries in our business offices. These girls should know that we understand that. Editors and proprietors of newspapers should be as fair in publishing the facts of Romanism as they are in publishing any other important item of news. Much of the threat-

13

ened boycott against a liberal press is pure bluff. Preachers are untrue to their calling when they refuse to condemn the essential immoralities of Catholicism on the ground that it is a Church that teaches it. Is sin sanctified because it is taught and practiced by a so-called Church? Would any Protestant minister who is true to his God condone lying and theft if they constituted an intrinsic part of Protestant Moral Theology? Did the prophets cover up evil because it was practiced by leaders of the Jewish Church? Let us beware of Catholic politicians. Any man who has been educated in a Catholic school is presumably a Catholic; the burden of proof rests on him to show that he is not. Until he denounces that rotten religion he should not expect to receive the vote of any Protestant who knows the Romish standards of morals; he should be required to come clean. We must resist being boycotted in business on account of religion. Let every religion depend on its moral code for acceptance or rejection in business or politics.

5. WHAT ARE THE SIGNS OF THE CONVERSION OF A CATHOLIC?

In general he will show the absence of the "earmarks" of paganism. Specifically:

1. He will show patience instead of wild rage and passion when discussing the doctrines of his Church. He will study the essentials of his own religion.

2. He will be free from ridiculous fears of the occult world. Purgatory will cease to be a thing of dread. He will not feel forever under the necessity of having

a priest near to hear his confession and to administer extreme unction when he is called to die.

3. He will gladly read and study his Bible; it will be a new and precious book to him. He will shake off his lethargy and find out for himself what God would teach him.

4. A converted Catholic will cease to evade the consequences of his religion. He will admit the fruits of Romanism in Romish countries and give due credit to Protestantism in Protestant and in Catholic countries.

These changes will enable him to coöperate with Evangelical Christians in all their humane and Christian efforts. His snobbishness will have departed.

The Scripture, "He that being often reproved hardeneth his neck, shall suddenly be destroyed, and that without remedy," applies to religions as well as to individuals. Romanism has been so often reproved and has hardened her neck so persistently that we need not be surprised to see her destroyed some day and that without remedy.

The Parable of the Good Samaritan is a clarion called to all Christendom. The Roman Catholic hierarchy has left its millions wounded and neglected along the journey of life; more than that, she has sent her own bandits out into the wildernesses of human life and inspired them to attack the souls and bodies of men. It is the business of Protestantism to minister to the suffering and the desperate. But our work is not done until we break up the thieves-gang. Now, after eighteen hundred years, England, a Protestant nation, will probably prevent, in large measure, the lawless raids which have been made in

Palestine against travelers on the Jericho road for perhaps three millenniums. In the same manner will the Protestant religion both relieve the distress caused by Romanism and break the priestly power and intrigue which exploit and wound helpless pilgrims on the journey of life.

The test of final salvation in the last day is given by Jesus as that of service. Those who help the hungry, the sick, the prisoner, and the stranger will be accepted; those who do not will be rejected. Romanism creates poverty, fosters disease, foments crime, and misleads immigrants. Christianity creates wealth, wipes out epidemics, lessens crime, and liberates immigrants. If we would feed the hungry, bless the sick, reform those who are in prison, and build strong personalities out of the strangers who come among us, we shall be compelled to encourage just those free institutions for which Protestant nations are famous. He who helps to eliminate from the world the virus of Romanism is thus far helping and blessing all those mentioned by Jesus Christ (Matt. xxv. 31–46) as needing human help.

We shall not concern ourselves mainly with the Catholic Church as such; she must die. We are interested principally in all those Catholic members who desire to live the Christian life. May the good and wise God, who has set his seal on democratic governments and on Evangelical Missions, break the chains of those vast multitudes who are yet held in the prison house of Papal Paganism!

CHAPTER VII

THE CONFLICT BETWEEN PROPHETISM AND THE PAPAL PRIESTHOOD

PACIFISM in religion is as reprehensible as it is in statecraft. There seems to be at the present time a propaganda in the United States in favor of "peace-at-any-price." To be consistent, he who opposes a righteous war for self-defense should seek to do away entirely with police protection; the one is as truly war as the other. If all war is wrong, we should never have had our Revolutionary War and the Allies should have submitted supinely to the demands of the Central Powers. Jesus Christ refused to exercise the office of a magistrate; did he therefore abolish the civil power? The climax of the Beatitudes is, "Blessed are the peacemakers." Millions of times conscientious sheriffs, judges, juries, and jailers have established peace in the face of outlawry; it often required arrest, imprisonment, trial, and hanging.

When, on the night of his betrayal, Jesus suggested to his disciples that they should arm themselves for the dangers which were soon to follow, and one of the disciples answered to the effect that they had two swords, he said, "It is enough." While they were to respect law as did their Master, there was no necessity to throw themselves recklessly into the hands of bandits. They were under the same obligation to oppose enemies of the law as they were to obey the law. By the proper use of the short sword, which

(197)

prudent men very naturally carried when in danger, they would be upholding the law.

Warfare for Christianity is of two sorts; material and spiritual. No man has a right to use the material sword to protect his belief; all men have a right to use force to protect their lives against those who in disobedience to the law seek to take their lives or destroy their property.

The Old Testament is very clear as to the duties of citizens to use force against criminals. The New Testament deals very little with that subject; it rather takes all that for granted. Since Jesus and his immediate followers were subjects of the Roman government and had little to do except to obey, there are no specific rules given as to voting, initiating reform movements, or declaring war.

The difference between Romanism and Christianity at this point is that the former meets argument with armory, ballots with bullets, and opposes brute force to moral character, while the latter meets physical force with physical force, if it is unavoidable, and falsehood with truth.

However indispensable it may sometimes be to repel force with force, no right-thinking man wants war. The only thing that will cure the world of war is the establishment of justice and liberty; this cannot be done by merely constructive work in righteousness. The symbol of the New Dispensation introduced by Jesus Christ was the human tongue. It was a tongue of flame on the great day of Pentecost which was to be used for the dissemination of truth. The printed page is only an extension of the faculty of speech. The disciples of Jesus are called by their

Master "the light of the world." It is the business of true ministers to bombard the citadels of darkness that the light may shine in.

At some future day there will probably be no need of fighting; at the present time all lovers of truth must "earnestly contend for the faith which was once delivered unto the saints." We, like the Psalmist, ought to say, "Blessed be the Lord my strength, which teacheth my hands to war, and my fingers to fight."

SHALL WE FIGHT ROMANISM?

Let us introduce this question with another: Shall we fight any other forms of evil? If it is our duty to expose and oppose any form of wickedness, why should it be our duty to make an exception of any given class of sin? If it is our duty to throw light on immorality in general, the burden of proof lies on him who objects to fighting Romanism to show that that system of corruption should be left out of the account.

Many timid souls avoid this subject for fear that they might be found fighting against God. We have seen that Romanism is anti-Christian according to her documents and that the principles enunciated in these anthentic utterances have actuated her for twenty-five centuries. It is certain that these laws have not been changed and that they cannot be changed.

Theologically Romanism is anti-Christian. She is polytheistic and idolatrous. She rules a vast majority of her people through fear of an invented purgatory and of a hell to which they are to be consigned if they should choose a righteous path and

live a correct life. She has deprived the most of her
people of the use of the Bible; sometimes by command, often by keeping it out of their reach, generally by placing it beyond them by high prices;
wherever possible, by keeping them in ignorance so
that they cannot read it. Even where she lets them
have it, the common people are discouraged by being
continually reminded that only the magically quali-
fied priesthood can understand it. Then, to make the
case desperate, she poisons this spring of knowledge
by vicious translations and notes and by other literature which contradicts it. Rome leads her people
into a wilderness of rites and ceremonies which nullify the efficacy of simple spontaneous prayer and
faith in a personal God. A priesthood has been thrust
into the New Testament dispensation contrary to
the will and purpose of Jesus Christ. An immoral
code has been elaborated until plain morality is
checkmated at every step. Meddling with civil
government is the practical outcome of it all.

THE UNITED STATES THE PRINCIPAL BATTLE GROUND OF ROMANISM

This seems to be the only country which has given
Romanism almost free rein in modern times. Two
things have resulted from this: (1) By constant contact with Protestants and liberals, many Catholics
here have developed a much higher type of character
than in most other countries; this has made it comparatively easy for the hierarchy to create the impres-
sion that Romanism has changed. (2) The priesthood has lost no time in laying their plans to make
America Catholic, while they continually put our

citizens to sleep to the lullaby of "tolerance," "Christian charity," "let everybody alone." The right settlement of the Catholic question in this country will affect powerfully the peace of the world for all time to come.

Virtually all the evils of this country have as their most powerful ally the Roman Catholic Church. In this monumental struggle the logical leaders are the priests on one side and the Christian ministry on the other.

Wave on wave of *gambling* sweeps over this country from time to time. While the desire to get something for nothing is an easy temptation to a majority of people, and while multitudes of Protestants bet and gamble with little or no qualm of conscience, yet the fact that the Catholic Church both sanctions and practices gambling is a most powerful factor in fomenting this spirit. Perhaps a majority of the Christian ministry are guilty of lending their silent aid to the doctrine and practice of Romanism at this point. No Christian minister is guiltless who refuses to expose the most fertile source of gambling we have in our nation. Over against the Protestant pulpit stands the Romish hierarchy aiding and abetting the enemies of good government.

Immigration is a most important matter to be settled by Americans. It would be absurd to say that we ourselves have no right to say who shall and who shall not come to this country. This is largely a Catholic question. For many years now we have been receiving great floods of people from Southern and Southeast Europe. Perhaps more than one-half of our immigrants for the past twenty years have

been Roman Catholics untrained in American ideals
and generally unwilling to be instructed. These
people feel obliged to obey their priests rather than
our laws. The most strenuous objectors to restriction of immigration to this country are the Romish
prelates. Why is this? To be sure, it is that the
Romanizing of America will be postponed or prevented if Rome is shut up to making converts from
Americans, especially in this era when Romanism is
being exposed so freely. Shall we ignore Romish
efforts in our plans to assimilate the aliens we now
have and our proposed legislation to make the task
easier?

The whole world is looking on to see how we shall
dispose of *the liquor traffic*. Rome has stood almost
solidly for one hundred years for the open saloon.
Now that we have a constitutional law prohibiting
it she is just as stubbornly against it as she ever was.
A prominent Catholic lawyer of New York has recently written a book which is an attack on the
Eighteenth Amendment to our Constitution. The
Knights of Columbus are out of sympathy with prohibition. Of all the twenty thousand priests in this
country, probably not over one per cent of them
labored to secure prohibition. Why is Rome opposed to prohibition? Because she is against our
Constitution itself. Moreover, there is so little moral
power in the Catholic Church that she is impotent to
advance the cause of total abstinence among either
priests or members. Besides, liquor enables the
priesthood to impede general education and clean
politics.

Education is fundamental to the progress of a nation. No wonder that a part of the Syllabus forbids the pope to reconcile himself to progress. Opposition to the Sterling-Reed bill in our Congress centers in Romanism. A pretext is made that it would interfere with State rights, while Rome has always favored a strong central government. The real reason is that it will mean to wipe out our disgraceful illiteracy. Mexico has been able to make some progress in education, but only as she forced the priests to keep their place. Rome, following her long-established custom of blaming everybody except herself, whines that she would have educated the people had not the government persecuted her. That is false. In Spain, Rome has had all the freedom she desired, yet we behold the spectacle there of seventy-eight per cent illiteracy with woeful indifference even among those who *can* read. Why do our Protestant ministers hedge and compromise on the educational question? If all our Churches and preachers would come out and denounce the un-American effort of Rome on this subject, we should be able to establish State education as it should be. We shall have to come to the principle of prohibiting parochial schools. Freedom of worship is fully granted when we permit a Church to teach from its pulpit and through its press the doctrines of the union of Church and State and the immoralities for which Rome stands. If the Church prefers not to use those channels and seeks to infiltrate such wicked doctrines among the innocent and unsuspecting youth, we as Americans must prevent it. Besides, if her doctrines cannot stand the light of day, we should be ashamed to help her inculcate them in ways which are virtually secret. Another pretext is

that the State denies the right of parents to have
their children educated religiously.   If Romish
priests would let their people alone, it would soon be
evident that the average Catholic father prefers the
public school to the parochial.   The issue here is not
between the Catholic family and the public school,
but between meddlesome priests and democratic
government.   The logical place for Christian ministers is on the side of the government, in favor of all
the youth and necessarily against the Romish hierarchy.

Americans are often guilty of *high finance*. We are
getting to be a nation of money-grubbers.   Avarice
is not peculiar to us; it is not a monopoly of the Catholic Church.   It did not originate in Rome.   Yet,
the example of thousands of priests seeking something
for nothing is bound to have its effect.   Masses for
souls in purgatory is fraud pure and simple.   Almsgiving as penance is a vain contribution to a greedy
priesthood.   If Romanists wish to spend their money
that way, they have a right to do it; but the example,
when not rebuked by liberals and Protestants, must
lead many to seek a similar method of getting money.
Besides, the doctrine of secret compensation is directly demoralizing on all who believe it.   Add to this
the Romish sanction of gambling, betting, and lotteries, and you have a great body of twenty million
people committed to a wicked system.   Such influence must inevitably lead to trickery in business.

Political dishonesty is a crying evil of our time in
the United States.   This is not confined to Romanists.   It would not vanish if Romanism should go out
of fashion.   The lobbies of Catholics in the capital is

not of itself wrong. But the lobbies are there. We ask, Why are they there? When we know what Romanism is, we can expect them to intrigue against our government. There are at present three hundred and eighty-three Protestants in the House of Representatives as against thirty-seven Catholics, and eighty-seven Protestants in the Senate while there are only five Catholics. How can we explain the fact that for five years the effort to give Federal aid to the States to abolish illiteracy has been held up? There have been enough Protestants there all the time to pass the bill calling for a Department of Education with its Secretary in the President's Cabinet and an appropriation of $100,000,000 to the different States. As soon as the bill was introduced Rome got busy.

The political guns of the Roman hierarchy instantly concentrated their fire on the proposal. Two hundred periodicals of the hierarchy in English and a hundred in foreign tongues devoted their front and editorial pages constantly to denunciation of the measure. More than ten thousand pulpits of the Roman Church joined in the chorus of bitter intolerant opposition. Fifty nation-wide fraternities of the papal system on our soil exploited resolutions of condemnation inspired by the hundred thrones of the hierarchy. Covert lobbying activities of Rome at the National capital redoubled their energy.

What was the result? Cowardly politicians took fright. It was unnecessary. Had they been true to their constituency and to their country, they would have passed the bill immediately. We are reminded by this one incident how much can be done by an unscrupulous anti-American religion. The matter is still up for consideration. It may be passed this time; if it is not, it will be mainly because of the subtlety of Rome, but not wholly. Our own Protestants are yielding to a thoroughly organized anti-patriotic religion and out of fear. Who shall arrest this downward trend of morals among our so-called statesmen? The citizenship is rising up against it now. If our pulpits would ring clear on such matters, the enemy could not get far. But Romish prelates have been long sowing the seeds of "tolerance" among Protestants while they continued their work of undermining our government.

The press of this country is notoriously venal on the subject of Romanism and of those reforms which require courage. It is impossible to get the most important facts on any subject which Rome has forbidden the papers to give publicity to. Such a condition of affairs has continued until it has become necessary for papers which definitely defend Americanism and Protestantism to make such work a specialty. Rome has efficiently muzzled the press of the United States. Even the hundreds of Protestant Church periodicals of the country have lent their silent influence to this propaganda. Often one will find an article in a Protestant Church organ commending Romanism.

When the springs of information are polluted or diverted, the country is in a bad way. It is positively criminal for the press to stand between the people and the facts which they should have. Who shall secure for our citizenship the data on which enlightened opinion is to be formed? It is passing strange that the pulpits and Church papers should permit such anti-American conduct without raising a protest.

Economic questions are deeply religious. Extreme socialism, communism, Bolshevism, and various other forms of protest against the misuse of capital find their best breeding places in countries cursed by priestcraft. Revolutions in Catholic countries are as natural and as necessary as the breaking of the eggshell when the chick is hatched. The rights of the poor man cannot be respected as long as Romanism reigns. Paganism is cruelty in the name of religion. Might makes right, according to heathen cults. The might of the priesthood aligns itself with that of the wealthy. This makes assurance doubly sure. The intelligent and the nobility are controlled by money; the poor and ignorant are controlled by superstitious fears and hopes. It is to the interest of priest and capitalist to keep down wages. High wages means independence, education, and power.

The present status of the hierarchy in the United States concerning education and economical questions is to papal priests perhaps the most trying they have ever experienced. Which way shall they turn? Whither shall they fly? Poor and illiterate Catholics can see the freedom which education gives to Protestant nations. They become convinced here in the United States that knowledge improves the lot of the poor. But Romanism has always exploited the common man. What shall she do now? With her usual cunning, Rome has temporarily solved the problem. By turning a stream of Irish priests to this country the fine Italian hand has done what could never have been done by Italian, French, German, or American priests. An Irishman is so endowed that he can see double and be sober at the same time. That is what

gives the flavor to an Irish bull. Archbishop Purcell
was born in Ireland. Cardinal Gibbons was educated in the Emerald Isle. An Irish Catholic bishop
could state that his Church had nothing hidden, that
she kept nothing back, that there was no freemasonry
in it, and appear as innocent as if he thought he were
telling the truth. No doubt Romish priests get some
enjoyment out of the readiness of Americans to take
their Irish jokes seriously. But they cannot feel
very complacent. The present movement to expose
the Romish code of morals and politics is not a spurt.
It is very similar to the Prohibition movement;
liquor men tried to believe that it was "another move
of fanaticism," but they came to themselves when
they saw the handwriting on the wall.

A growing contempt for law is most alarming in this
country. This is not an accident. There are
causes; chief among them is the attitude of the Roman Catholic hierarchy to our whole system of government. It is impossible for a true Catholic priest to
believe in the fundamentals of our Constitution.
The hatred of the priests for our freedom must be
communicated to "strong Catholics." The closer a
Romanist is to his priest, the farther he is from American ideals. Why do we kill so many people and why
are so few of the guilty punished? When Catholics
can with impunity form mobs and stone and murder
Protestants who are in peaceable assembly, it would
seem that the Protestant pulpit would cry aloud and
spare not. Such lawless practices will continue until
the conscience of the nation is aroused and until the
light is thrown on the intrigues of alien Roman
enemies who live among us and enjoy our hospitality.

Every confessional box is likely on occasion to be used against any law for the advancement of good government. The Romish clergy has always used its power through the secret of the confessional to the hurt of free nations.

Why do we have fully ten times as many homicides per population as they have in England and do not punish one-tenth of the guilty ones, while England punishes practically all of those who commit that crime? There are various causes. It may be said that we are a new nation, a pioneer in democratic government, having hordes of unassimilated foreigners. Our gigantic and rapid increase of material wealth has stimulated materialism and pride. There is a lawless element in human nature which lies at the bottom of all sin and crime. But all these explanations do not exhaust the subject.

The Roman Catholic doctrines and polity, as shown by Romish documents all illustrated in history, are such as to condemn that system. Who intrigues to bring the unassimilable foreigners here? Who tries to see that our democratic government is a failure? If the whole Roman hierarchy hates our very constitution, may we expect the average layman to love and inwardly respect the laws that are based on that constitution? Who is it that fights and despises freedom of speech and of peaceable assembly? It is getting now to be a daily occurrence that lecturers on Americanism should be prevented from speaking either in public halls or on the streets. It will not be long before preachers and their congregations will be stoned because pulpits are used to expose Romish idolatry, the Catholic code of morals, and

14

the Romish hatred of free government. This would
be done now if any considerable number of preachers
should dare to tell their people the truth concerning
Romanism.

If we are to preach no more against sin, it must be
either because human nature has so changed since
the Bible was written that men can no more be won
from wickedness to righteousness by having their
iniquities exposed or else the whole of our Sacred
Scripture is wrong. Has human nature changed radically during the last two thousand years? I grant
that there has been some improvement. Comparatively few tribes now eat human flesh; many thousands of savages have lost their appetite for that sort
of food. Legalized torture is not used any more in
decent nations and there is a growing aversion to it.
Parental ownership has passed out and parents do
not care to maim or kill their children. The world
seems to be aroused to the possibility of banishing
strong drink. But we have avarice, lust, unholy
ambition, hatred of light and liberty, bloodthirsti-
ness, lying, etc., almost as rampant as they ever were.

WHAT IS SACERDOTALISM?

We do not here discuss the priesthood of the Old
Testament. There was a place for that order in the
economy of the Jews. It never stood as high as that
of the prophets. It was hereditary, and for that reason, if for no other, it had to degenerate. The priest
in New Testament times, especially in this era of
light, is not simply antagonistic to a higher morality
as he was so frequently in Israel. The very nature of
the priestly office is necessarily destructive; only by

the most desperate methods can it now gain recognition among intelligent people. The source of its power is brought out now into the fierce light of science. "The essence of sacerdotalism," says Mr. Sheldon, "lies in a profound emphasis on priestly authority and on sacramental efficacy. The name is indicative of the system which exalts the office of the priestly hierarchy and the virtue of the rites supposed to depend for their valid administration upon that hierarchy."[1]

That Roman sacerdotalism is coming to be a greater menace than it has been since the Reformation seems to be the opinion of that great theologian. The author continues:

The spirit, purpose, and action of priestly hierarchies were never surcharged more deeply than at present with an intense hatred of that evangelical teaching which emphasizes the freedom and responsibility of the individual in the sphere of religious belief and practice. If that teaching is to maintain itself, it must be at the expense of earnest warfare. . . . The champion of the evangelical standpoint who responds to the claims of sacerdotalism with nothing better than a shake of the head, a shrug of the shoulders, or an expression of contempt, simply advertises his own shallowness. His method is too closely akin to the sacerdotal plan of refuting by anathemas to claim a grain of respect.

The Greeks winked at the orgies and moral turpitude of their gods on the ground that they belonged to such high ranks of being that they were not to be held accountable to the ordinary rules of human morality. Will Catholics forever excuse their priests for the same reason? It is not likely.

---

[1] "Sacerdotalism in the Nineteenth Century," by Henry C. Sheldon.

WHAT IS PROPHETISM?

A prophet is one who speaks for God, but he must first set an example of right living. His crowning work is that of saving souls from the power of sin by presenting to them the truth of God both by precept and example. Prophets in the early history of Israel were often called seers. It is said in the Hebrew Bible, "Where there is no vision, the people perish." That is also true in every nation and in every period of history. A prophet is *called* and *sent*. A priest comes from the people. Scripture says, "And there shall be, like people, like priest;" such men seldom initiate reforms. Prophets hear the call of God and bring to men the message for which they are divinely sent. "There was a man sent from God, whose name was John." He called multitudes to repentance. When a prophet becomes a trimmer, he is no more a prophet. When Jonah was sent to Nineveh, the Lord said to him: "Arise, go to Nineveh, and preach unto it the preaching that *I bid thee*." A story is told in 1 Kings xiii. of a prophet who was sent to King Jeroboam at Bethel to testify against his wickedness and idolatry. The task was performed successfully, but the prophet made the mistake of neglecting his further duty of returning to his home immediately. On the advice of a fellow prophet he disobeyed his Lord by spending the night with his friend. On the day following, this unfaithful man of God was slain by a lion on his way home. Let prophets beware lest they hear another voice than that of their Sender.

While every true minister of the gospel is a prophet, the gift is not confined to them. Real statesmen also speak to men in the name and by the help of God. W. E. Gladstone, George Washington, Abraham Lincoln, and Benito Juarez heard and heeded the voice of God and gave his truth to men. Poets listen to celestial music and interpret it to the world. Dante, Milton, Tennyson, and Browning lifted men above sordid things and helped them to see the invisible. Philosophers may belong to the prophetic succession. Solomon, Socrates, Benjamin Franklin, and Francis Bacon taught their fellows the higher way of life.

The glory of prophetism is that it may be dispensed among all who are willing to receive it, it makes divine things intensely human. It levels up. After the wonderful Pentecostal shower Peter explained that it was the beginning of a new era, an era in which servants (slaves) were to be filled with the Holy Spirit and with the gift of speaking for God, with the power of God dwelling in them.

The difference between the prophet and the priest is, in a word, that the essence of the prophet's power *is shared* by the disciple, whereas the priestly power of magic is his own in a peculiar way; when it is delivered on the devotee it has lost its fecundity; it can never be transmitted any further. The faculty of saving souls is the special possession of the priest; the ordinary Catholic can do nothing to save souls; he can only persuade men to come to the priest. The evangelical Christian may transmit the grace of God exactly as does his prophet.

We are told by some of our fellow Protestants that we should love Catholics into the kingdom and not fight them. The implication is that if we expose the iniquities of the priests who are doing their worst to keep the light of Holy Scripture away from their devotees we are fighting the members of the Catholic Church, and if we are fighting them it is because we do not love them. If that be true, John the Baptist fought and hated the people whose sins he denounced. How can their repentance be explained? Is it likely that multitudes would have heard the Baptist had he been filled with bitterness toward them? Can we accuse Jesus of not loving the common people into the kingdom because, forsooth, he fiercely rebuked the sins of those demons who were exploiting them? For fear that we shall be accused of hate, shall we refuse to declare *all* the "counsel of God"? "He that hateth reproof is brutish." Shall we fail to reprove because some will hate us? Shall we shirk duty because we are accused of not loving those whom we would help? "Faithful are the wounds of a friend; but the kisses of an enemy are deceitful."

There is a feeling among some people that Catholics are not always consistent with their doctrines and are therefore good citizens and even sometimes Christians, while Protestants are often inconsistent with their doctrines and are therefore no better than average Catholics. The logic is that Romanists are naturally so good that the iniquitous doctrines of their religion do not materially injure their character, while Protestants are naturally so bad that the higher morality of their religion does them very little good. Such reasoning is to deny our own principles that Bible-reading and the hearing of sermons setting forth the moral code of Christ have no appreciable effect for good. It also ignores facts. We have demonstrated that deep poverty, political graft, drunkenness, gambling, disease, illiteracy, weakness in government, etc., are the inevitable results in all those countries where Rome has large sway. If we do not find these evils standing out clearly where Romanists are scattered among Protestants, that itself is proof of the superiority of Evangelical Christianity.

The story is told of a little boy who wrote a composition on pins. Said he: "A pin is a small instrument, with a round head and a sharp point. Pins are made of brass. Women use many pins. Pins have saved thousands of lives." "What!" said the teacher; "how do pins save so many lives?" The boy retorted: "By not swallowing them." The only way that Romanism can save men from sin is by their not swallowing it.

I heard a Protestant minister say: "If Romanism had not a great deal of good in it, God would have kicked it out of existence long ago." That is putting a good deal of responsibility on the sovereignty of God. Does Jehovah kick out of existence everything that is wrong? Savagery has not been kicked out of existence and it has continued for a long time. What has the Almighty done in that case? He has continued for millenniums to let savages eat one another. And they will probably continue with their cruel and superstitious rites until the people of God change them by giving them the truth which is not heard without a preacher. Neither are God's ministers to kick out of existence idolatry and the priesthood; they are to throw light on all sorts of sin, but more especially those sorts which are the most fatal and which injure the largest number of people.

We may be told that the Hebrew prophets rebuked apostate and recreant Hebrew priests who knew better, while we are dealing with priests who are conscientious. This would apply to Buddhist priests. In dealing with the leaders of those religions which do not claim to be Christian everything which may be regarded as common ground should be emphasized. This method cannot be followed in dealing with arrogant Romish priests. It has never yet succeeded. The best Christian missionaries among Catholics are clear-cut in presenting the gospel. This has been tested. Ever and anon a new missionary or bishop or executive or missionary specialist endeavors to set us an example of "coöperation with the sincere and well-meaning" Catholic priests. Experienced missionaries to Catholics have only to smile and wait.

ADVANCEMENT IN RELIGION HAS ALWAYS BEEN EFFECTED THROUGH CONFLICT

The religion of the Old Testament was based on prophetism. Abraham was rather a prophet than a priest; indeed he was contrasted with a priest, Melchizedec, by the author of the Epistle to the Hebrews (Heb. vii. 1-7), to the advantage of the father of the faithful, notwithstanding the high position of Melchizedec. It was Moses the prophet, not Aaron the high priest, who organized Israel and gave to them the great system of moral, spiritual, and civil laws.

The period of greatest spiritual power and glory among the Jews was that in which their great prophets were functioning. The philippics, hurled by all those spiritual giants against idolatry, ceremonialism, oppression, infidelity, and vileness, brought about continual resentment from the comfortable and the ruling classes. How any one can read the seventeen prophetical books of the Old Testament and condone idolatry, with its priesthood and its iniquitous code of ethics, can be explained only on the ground that he has been deceived, or else that he has revised the Bible doctrine concerning these sins.

The New Dispensation was ushered in by the trumpet call of a prophet, John the Baptist. He was a born fighter. He did not drive the people away from God, nor from righteousness, nor even from himself. Some preachers are like the court minister who said in preaching before the king, "All men are mortal;" on seeing that the king was displeased, he then stated, "Some men are mortal." At that the king was completely disgusted.

Jesus Christ was called Prophet, Priest, and King. As King he is supreme and needs no royal representative on earth. He never sanctioned the "divine right of kings." As Priest he was the antitype and final fulfillment of all previous priesthoods. As Prophet, however, he was both the fulfillment of prophecy and the Exemplar, Lord, Teacher, and Companion of all prophets who should come after him. Nothing is said in the New Testament about Apostolic Succession, but all those who are persecuted for righteousness' sake are in the Succession of the Prophets. "Rejoice and be exceeding glad," said Jesus to that sort of people, "for so persecuted they the *prophets* which were before you."

"We should treat Catholics in a Christlike manner," is the counsel we sometimes receive. What do our friends mean by that? Let them read again Matthew xxiii. Jesus called those men who were exploiting the unsuspecting, "fools," "hypocrites," "blind guides," "whited sepulchers," a "generation of vipers," and winds up by saying, "How can ye escape the damnation of hell?" Was that a Christlike manner? Perhaps we shall be told that since Jesus was the Son of God he had a right to say things that we, his human followers, cannot say. But how are we to find out what the "Christlike manner" is unless we get it from our guide?

The apostle Paul was no more a deity than we are. Read his description of some eminent foe of Christianity (2 Thess. ii. 3–12). He is called "that wicked," "whose coming is after the working of Satan with all power and signs and lying wonders." The same apostle said to Elymas the sorcerer: "O full of all subtlety and all mischief, thou child of the devil."

But the unthinking defenders of Rome are not easily convinced. Another turn is taken. "Those apostles had a peculiar right to condemn sin and expose sinners; we are not so high up in the ranks of the ministry as they; men since those days must be more conciliatory." Had Martin Luther had the voice of a cooing dove, we would to-day (so far as we can now see) have been groveling in the mire of superstition and bowing our necks to the successors of Hildebrand and Alexander VI.

If we would meet the deadliest foe of righteousness, we should reflect again on the terrific conflicts through which Christianity has already come. We

shall do well to go back a century or two and listen
to the clarion call of the men of God who met the
enemy undaunted. The prophetic note needs to be
sounded again among us.

Let us ponder over the vivid description of the
ravages of Romanism given by a great poet of former
days:

"O love-destroying, cursed bigotry!
  Cursed in heaven, but cursed more in hell,
  Where millions curse thee and must ever curse!
  Religion's most abhorred, perdition's most
  Forlorn! God's most abandoned! hell's most damned!
  The infidel who turned his impious war
  Against the walls of Zion, on the rock
  Of ages built, and higher than the clouds,
  Sinned and received his due reward; but she
  Within her walls sinned more. Of ignorance
  Begot, her daughter, Persecution, walked
  The earth from age to age, and drank the blood
  Of God's peculiar children, and was drunk,
  And in her drunkenness dreamed of doing good.
  The supplicating hand of innocence,
  That made the tiger mild, and in his wrath
  The lion pause, the groans of suffering most
  Severe, were nought to her; she laughed at groans.
  No music pleased her more, and no repast
  So sweet to her as men of blood redeemed
  By blood of Christ. Ambition's self, though mad,
  And nursed on human gore, with her compared,
  Was merciful. Nor did she always rage;
  She had some hours of meditation, set
  Apart, wherein she to her study went.
  The Inquisition, model most complete
  Of perfect wickedness, where deeds were done—
  Deeds! let them ne'er be named—and sat and planned
  Deliberately and with most musing pains,
  How to extremest thrill of agony,
  The flesh, and blood, and souls of holy men,

Her victims, might be wrought; and when she saw
New tortures of her laboring fancy born,
She leaped for joy, and made great haste to try
Their force—well pleased to hear a deeper groan." [2]

But what of those who supinely submit to the blasphemous demands of Romish priests?

"Of those forlorn and sad, thou mightst have marked
In number most innumerable stand
The indolent; too lazy these to make
Inquiry for themselves, they stuck their faith
To some well-fatted priest with offerings bribed
To bring them oracles of peace, and take
Into his management and the concerns
Of their eternity; managed how well
They knew, that day, and might have sooner known
That the commandment was, Search, and believe
In me and not in man; who leans on him
Leans on a broken reed, that will impierce
The trusted side. I am the way, the truth,
The life, alone, and there is none besides.
This did they read and refused to search,
To search what easily was found, and, found,
Of price uncountable. Most foolish, they
Thought God with ignorance pleased, and blinded faith
That took not root in reason, purified
With holy influence of his Spirit pure.
So, on they walked, and stumbled in the light
Of noon, because they would not open the eyes.
Effect how sad of sloth, that made them risk
Of piloting to the eternal shore,
To one who could mistake the lurid flash
Of hell for heaven's true star, rather than bow
The knee, and by one fervent word obtain
His guidance sure, who calls the stars by name."

In view of the vicious Catholic moral code, the use of it in all Romish history and realizing the unques-

---

[2] Pollok's "Course of Time."

tionable guilt of the priests, we must believe that
Paul's description of certain classes in his day and in
the days just ahead of him apply to the Romish
priesthood to-day as if he were making a portrait of
them.[3] The great Apostle warns:

This know also, that in the last days perilous times shall
come. For men shall be lovers of their own selves, covetous,
boasters, proud, blasphemers, disobedient to parents, unthankful, unholy, without natural affection, trucebreakers,
false accusers, incontinent, fierce, despisers of those that are
good, traitors, heady, highminded [self-important—*Modern
Speech N. T.*], lovers of pleasures more than lovers of God.
. . . For of this sort are they which creep into houses, and
lead captive silly women laden with sins, led away with divers
lusts, ever learning and never able to come to the knowledge
of the truth. Now as Jannes and Jambres withstood Moses,
so do these also resist the truth; men of corrupt minds, reprobate concerning the faith.

If the reader will examine carefully each detail in
the above delineation, he will realize how true it is as
to the Teaching Body of Romanism. Even the
phrase "disobedient to parents" fits them when we
consider the kind of obedience a priest must render
to his superiors. Without doubt those honest moth-
ers who have been deceived into surrendering their
precious boys into the hands of the Church would
deprecate the guilt of their sons where they stain
their hands with human gore to advance the interests of "Holy Mother." It is significant that this
unholy stepmother, the Church, should require the
renunciation of all those pure principles which every
good human mother has planted in the minds of her
sons.

---

[3] 2 Timothy iii. 1–8.

Catholic priests are unthankful to those countries which give them freedom to carry on their intrigues; especially is this true in the United States. Blasphemy is the essence of the papacy. Priests are warned by their theologians to banish natural affection from their hearts so far as wives and children are concerned. The whole Inquisition is blackened with false accusations; just such accusations as were brought by Old Rome against the early Christians. To break faith with a heretic is specifically required not only of the priest but of the "faithful." The incontinence of priests is almost universal in Latin America. Priestly ferocity is seen on every hand; this is carefully inculcated in the minds of their members. A priest must be a traitor to any country whenever his pope demands it. No Romish priest can believe in the fundamentals of the Constitution of the United States. Mexico knows well that the whole hierarchy has always been an enemy to the liberty of that Republic. It is specifically stated by Romish theologians that the confessional makes it easy for the priest to seduce women, either directly or by making appointments to meet them at other times and places. It is notorious how priests resist the truth.

The fight is on. Let no one fear lest he should precipitate something. The two systems—the Christian and the sacerdotal—are irreconcilable. Romanism as the goal of all pagan systems is on trial, perhaps once for all. If Christianity is the absolute religion, it will have to rise to its responsibility or let the world go back into another night. I am aware that science is advancing, but religion is far deeper than science. Human hate and ignorance can blot out whole civilizations. Intelligence is very far from universal yet, and it cannot become universal unless some solid principle of morals and religion be reached. If Christ has not given us a platform of spiritual religion and unselfish morality, there is none.

Eclecticism in morals or religion is a failure. The Jews are an example of a people who have vainly tried to live an ethical life without a deep religious foundation.

No substantial reform can be made which has not its roots deeply planted in the past. We need to go back to the reformers and, still further back, to the struggles of the dissident sects and to primitive Christianity. The world needs Christianity now as much as it ever did, and more. If we are to be thrown into the most intimate relations with all nations and peoples and tongues, we must have a common basis on which to meet.

Christianity is necessarily aggressive. Macaulay has pointed out the most "remarkable fact, that no Christian nation which did not adopt the principles of the Reformation before the end of the sixteenth century should ever have adopted them." Says he: "Catholic communities have, since that time, become infidel and become Catholic again; but none has become Protestant."

We need to return to the spirit of Knox and Luther, of Huss and Savonarola, of Paul and John the Baptist. And when we sit again at the feet of Jesus, may we not hope to catch his spirit?